369 4955

Our Compassionate Savior

Gospel Images for Prayer

LUKE

by Robert L. Knopp

Foreword by Robert F. Morneau

Pauline
BOOKS & MEDIA

Nihil Obstat:
Rev. Thomas W. Buckley, STD, SSL

Imprimatur:
†Bernard Cardinal Law
Archbishop of Boston
June 10, 1996

Cover design: Sergia Ballini, FSP

ISBN 0-8198-3087-9

Printed and published in the U.S.A. by Pauline Books & Media, 50 Saint Pauls Avenue, Boston MA 02130-3491.

http://www.pauline.org

Pauline Books & Media is the publishing house of the Daughters of St. Paul, an international congregation of women religious serving the Church with the communications media.

1 2 3 4 5 6   03 02 01 00 99 98

Contents

Foreword

A fierce battle is taking place in our culture regarding the imagination. Nor is this a *cold* war but one of extreme passion and intensity. The importance of victory cannot be exaggerated because the images we create or absorb shape our inner attitudes, which in turn radically influence our lifestyle and behavior. It's a simple syllogism but one which has profound ramifications.

Images come from multiple sources: television, songs, movies, magazines, science, poetry, lived lives. Within the Christian community a major source stimulating the imagination is sacred Scripture. God's word often draws pictures for us that contain values and virtues that lead us to the kingdom: Jesus as good shepherd; our spirituality as one of mutual self-giving as depicted in the vine and the branches; the separation of the sheep and the goats based on our treatment of one another; God as the potter shaping and molding our lives.

In a world filled with incredible violence, the Christian community continues to offer an alternative to the culture of death. Ours is to be a culture of love, a "civilization of love," in which every single human being is invited to the wedding feast and must be treated with awesome respect. The poet Gerard Manley Hopkins calls us "immortal diamonds." Our images must offer realistic hope.

It is not enough to encounter an image, symbol, metaphor or story. More is required. We must assimilate and appropriate these formative sights and sounds until they are absorbed into our spiritual bloodstream. This will require prayer and reflection as well as commitment to translate them into action. Our process of formation and conversion takes time and much grace. Perseverance in prayer is essential to Christian maturity.

This volume, like its three companions, is about discipleship and how we respond to that call by using biblical images. Robert Knopp looks deeply into each of the Gospels and extracts for us images that give us access to the person of Jesus. Each Gospel is unique in its approach to the Lord but all are the same in inviting us to know, love and serve him with all of our being.

In *Our Compassionate Savior,* Jesus is manifest as our forgiving, tender, empathetic Lord. Embedded in the Christian imagination are the images of the prodigal son and his loving father, Jesus crying over Jerusalem, the portrayal of shepherds and widows and women gently treated. The Jesus of Luke heals, weeps, consoles, forgives, loves. To encounter this compassionate Lord in faith and prayer is to be changed forever.

One last word about images, the cornerstone of this book. Amos Niven Wilder, in his classic *Theopoetics,* writes: "It was urged that individuals and groups live by their images and dreams, and that it is harder to change the archetypes, symbols and myths of men than it is to change their ideas and doctrines." Luke's Gospel has forever changed our idea and doctrine of God by giving us a compassionate Jesus.

†Robert F. Morneau
Auxiliary Bishop of Green Bay

Invitation

L et's read together Luke's Gospel to find Jesus in our prayer, as Vatican II urged:

Learn by frequent reading of the divine Scriptures the "excellent knowledge of Jesus Christ" (Phil 3:8).... Prayer should accompany the reading of sacred Scripture, so that God and man may talk together; for "we speak to him when we pray; we hear him when we read the divine saying" (*Dogmatic Constitution on Divine Revelation*, no. 25, quoting St. Ambrose).

This little book, like its predecessors, *Mark: A Very Human Jesus* and *Matthew: Our Healing God-With-Us*, concentrates on the images—expressed or implied—in which the Gospel presents Jesus and his message. For, more than abstractions, images stir our hearts to pray.

Imagery usually appeals to our senses through rich color, form and sound, but the evangelists offer us no descriptive details of Jesus' external appearance and few such images of his actions. They prefer the symbolic imagery of narratives and parables that suggest the spiritual sense or inner mystery of Jesus' life, words and actions. To penetrate progressively into the mystery of Christ revealed in Luke's Gospel, I have divided it into units in which a key image or cluster of images can stir our musing and prayer. Then in rhythmic sense lines intended to harmonize with Luke's tone, I reflect on the inner meaning of his images to elicit a prayerful personal response.

Luke is the evangelist who most dearly loves and best masters the art of narration. Had he written in another era, instead of using the brief episodes (pericopes) typical of the Gospels, he might have cast his narratives in the form of ballads, blank verse, free verse or short stories. He considered his facts important in themselves, but even more important in their meaning; therefore he handled them more freely than would a modern journalist. Often more freely than Mark or Matthew, he interpreted the facts theologically and selected them according to the situation of his readers. In his prologue he tells Theophilus he is writing "that you may know the truth." In his epilogue, the Acts of the Apostles, he illustrates how he conveys these theological truths by the variations in his three accounts of Paul's conversion, each adapted to distinct audiences (see Acts 9:1-9; 22:1-11; 26:9-18). Luke's literary freedom suggests that as his readers we too may exercise our Christian freedom, guided by the Spirit, in selecting certain images and literary forms rather than others to inspire and express our prayer.

Within this freedom we must apply hermeneutic principles to understand more deeply what Luke was saying for his time and how it applies to ours. One such principle directs us to read his narratives within the literary form he chose, which is not a journalistic narrative to convey factually exact details, but a gospel narrative or parable to suggest the mystery of Jesus. Our lead question, then, is not to what extent a particular narrative is factual, but what it reveals about the inner meaning of Jesus' life. Another important principle directs us to read in context, in accord with our faith that the Holy Spirit inspired all the biblical writers and does not contradict himself, despite any appearances to the contrary. A third principle applies especially to difficult passages. We must keep in mind the general purpose of all sacred Scripture: to reveal the absolute goodness of God, whose infinite mercy Luke's Jesus reveals in his own compassion. In his *Life of Moses*, Gregory of Nyssa offers a classic application of this principle: anything in sacred Scripture that in its literal sense would be unworthy of God must have some hidden inner meaning. Thus, when Luke quotes Jesus as saying:

"Whoever comes to me and does not hate father and mother...yes, and even life itself, cannot be my disciple" (14:26), he does not mean that Jesus is commanding us to hate our parents or our life, but to love God more. Since Luke's Jesus quotes the commandment of love of parents in 18:20, he must mean in 14:26 that the great love we owe our parents is but "hate" compared to the greater love we owe God. Matthew helps us grasp Luke's strong expression by his own milder version: "Whoever loves father or mother more than me is not worthy of me" (Mt 10:37).

According to the leading source theory of biblical scholars, Mark wrote first; then Matthew and Luke repeated, summarized, expanded or revised nearly all his content as a primary source for their Gospels. Since I have already explored Mark's and Matthew's images, I have resisted repeating them here, except where necessary to maintain context and coherence, or where Luke introduces substantial changes. This decision allows us to focus upon what is original in Luke's Gospel, especially his dominant image of Jesus as the compassionate Savior of the outcast, the neglected, and women, who were so subordinated to the men of his day.

Luke prepares us for this special emphasis by his opening narratives of the birth and youth of Jesus among the poor, from whom God chooses the humble Virgin Mary to mother his Son, and reveals his identity to lowly shepherds. Luke's Jesus begins his ministry by presenting himself as the compassionate Servant of God foretold by Isaiah (40:3-5). Moved by a widow's tears, he restores to life her only son. He presents the Good Samaritan as model of compassion, even for fallen enemies. He depicts God as the Father who forgives both his prodigal son and his proud son with a love revealed in Jesus himself weeping over Jerusalem.

Luke's concentration on the compassion of Jesus often shines through the changes he makes in passages he uses from Mark. For example, he converts Mark's description of Jesus cursing a fig tree into a parable in which he asks his Father to let him cultivate the barren tree for another year. Into Mark's basic account of the passion, Luke inserts at least five images of Jesus rising above his own sufferings in his compassionate love for others, especially sinners: he heals the ear of one of his attackers, turns to call back the disciple who has denied him, consoles the women weeping over his suffering, prays for his executioners, and promises heaven to the good thief who accompanies him in death.

Besides portraying Jesus as our compassionate Savior, Luke makes other contributions to the gospel message by emphasizing Jesus' constant prayer to the Father, his obedience to the Holy Spirit, his unparalleled wisdom and his joyful embrace of life.

In the relatively few passages over which Christian churches still differ, I have adhered to the Catholic Church's interpretation of the apostolic traditions that gave rise to the New Testament. Though the Church has rarely interpreted individual verses, it provides an overall understanding of Scripture through the kerygma and its corollary doctrines, roughed out by the apostles themselves (as suggested in Acts 15 and some later passages of the New Testament, such as 2 Pt 1:16-21 and 3:16), and refined by the early Fathers of the Church and the councils.

I lovingly dedicate this book to my wife Marian, always the dearest partisan of my efforts.

Now enter with me into Luke's Gospel to ponder one image or group of images each day, letting it grow into prayer. As we begin, let's ask St. Luke to pray for us and invoke the Holy Spirit, to inspire us to find Luke's compassionate Savior.

The
Infancy Narrative

Prologue

Luke 1:1-4: *Since many have undertaken to set down an orderly account of the events that have been fulfilled among us, just as they were handed on to us by those who from the beginning were eyewitnesses and servants of the word, I too decided, after investigating everything carefully from the very first, to write an orderly account for you, most excellent Theophilus, so that you may know the truth concerning the things about which you have been instructed.*

To contemplate:

O Luke, could you see down the years
    the importance of these events
for the lives of the future people of God—
    for our lives here and now?
Not only for your Theophilus,
    but for all the lovers of God,
your careful research bears great fruit,
    for you tell us of his Son.

We picture you with your dear friend Paul,
    as he makes an urgent point;
we hear you question Peter and John,
    and disciples they have taught.
The early Christians so highly prized
    your search for the holy truth,
they included yours among the works
    they held as their sacred books.

You teach us care in searching out
    the truth about our Lord,
the implications of his acts,
    the meaning of his words.
The love with which you traced his love
    remade you into a saint!
Saint Luke, now help us penetrate
    the depths of your Gospel text.
To increase our knowledge of Jesus Christ,
    we will read your words with care;
to increase our love of our saving Lord,
    we will read his words in prayer.
Saint Luke, help us now appropriate
    your love for the Son of God.

O Lord, through Luke reveal to us
    your compassionate sacred heart!

God's Promise of His Prince

Lk 1:5-25: *In the days of King Herod of Judea, there was a priest named Zechariah.... There appeared to him an angel of the Lord.... The angel said to him, "Do not be afraid.... Your wife Elizabeth will bear you a son, and you will name him John.... Even before his birth he will be filled with the Holy Spirit. He will turn many of the people of Israel to the Lord their God. With the spirit and power of Elijah he will go before him...to make ready a people prepared for the Lord." Zechariah said to the angel, "How will I know that this is so? For I am an old man, and my wife is getting on in years." The angel replied, "I am Gabriel. I stand in the presence of God, and I have been sent...to bring you this good news. But now, because you did not believe my words...you will become mute...until the day these things occur...."*

After those days his wife Elizabeth conceived, and for five months she remained in seclusion. She said, "This is what the Lord has done for me when he looked favorably on me and took away the disgrace I have endured among my people."

To contemplate:

O Zechariah, why do you doubt
    the words of Gabriel?
As a priest of God can you doubt his might
    to perform a miracle?
In your preoccupation with one detail
    do you miss the angelic news—
good news that you will beget a son
    who will prepare for the Lord himself?

A message wrapped in mystery—
    the Lord of the world now comes!
To reveal his plan, he sends the one
    whom Daniel saw with fright (Dan 8:17):
Gabriel gave him a hint of the time
    when God would save his people
sending them "an anointed prince" (Dan 9:25)—
    don't you remember that?
How could you, so old and wise,
    doubt great Gabriel's word
as the word of God relayed to you
    of great events to come?

Though Zechariah is struck dumb,
    his aging wife conceives.
God's blessing blots out her "disgrace"—
    she conceives the prince's herald.
O God of great, mysterious plans,
    prepare us for your prince.

The Lord Is with You!

Lk 1:26-34: *In the sixth month [of Elizabeth's pregnancy] the angel Gabriel was sent by God to a town in Galilee called Nazareth, to a virgin engaged to a man whose name was Joseph, of the house of David. The virgin's name was Mary. And he came to her and said, "Greetings, favored one! The Lord is with you." But she was much perplexed by his words and pondered what sort of greeting this might be. The angel said to her, "Do not be afraid, Mary, for you have found favor with God. And now, you will conceive in your womb and bear a son, and you will name him Jesus. He will be great, and will be called the Son of the Most High, and the Lord God will give to him the throne of his ancestor David. He will reign over the house of Jacob forever, and of his kingdom there will be no end." Mary said to the angel, "How can this be, since I am a virgin?"*

To contemplate:

Now God's archangel Gabriel
   appears with his greatest news.
He has prepared noble Daniel
   and Zechariah the priest;

now he proclaims to a humble maid,
   "Greetings, O favored one!
The almighty Lord of heaven and earth
   is dwelling here with you!"

What can this young virgin think
   of "the Lord's favored one"?
In a race in which it is disgrace
   not to have a child,
how can she be God's "favored one"
   with whom the Lord abides?

Gabriel descends from his dignity
   to reassure the maid:
"Be not afraid, God blesses you
   to mother his own Son!"
How could Mary not rejoice
   at news of such a son?
Instead she asks: "How can this be,
   since I am a virgin maid?"

Yes, but a virgin engaged to a man—
   Joseph you are to wed.
Mary, what is God now asking of you
   through great Gabriel's word?
Are you to be both virgin and mother?
   How will you reply?

I Am the Servant of the Lord!

Lk 1:35-38: *The angel said to her, "The Holy Spirit will come upon you, and the power of the Most High will overshadow you; therefore the child to be born will be holy; he will be called Son of God. And now, your relative Elizabeth in her old age has also conceived a son; and this is the sixth month for her who was said to be barren. For nothing will be impossible with God." Then Mary said, "Here am I, the servant of the Lord; let it be with me according to your word." Then the angel departed from her.*

To contemplate:

"How can a virgin conceive a child?"

"God will send his Spirit to you,
to incarnate his Son of your very flesh!
    As his cloud once covered Moses' tent,
he will enfold you in his own warm love (Ex 40:34)—
    creative presence of Trinity.
For now, Mary, you're invited to be
    the tabernacle of his only Son.

As Elizabeth, in her great old age,
    will have a very special child,
so you, though virgin, can bear God's Son—
    for nothing is beyond our God!"

O Mary, what will you answer God,
    the God who humbly now proposes:
"Will you bear for me my own dear Son,
    bear him as a member of your race?"
The God of heaven humbles himself
    before the humble virgin Mary,
sends Gabriel, his mighty messenger,
    to ask her to bear his only Son,
and thus fulfill to David his pledge:
    "Your greatest heir will be my Son"
    (2 Sam 7:12-14).

O Mary, what will you answer God?
    Will you doubt his Gabriel's solemn word,
    even as Zechariah did?

The whole world listens for your reply,
    stops in breathless anxiety:
"Here am I, the Lord's own servant;
    I lovingly embrace his word!"

    Your Lord becomes your son!

Blessed Are You among Women

Lk 1:39-45: *In those days Mary set out and went with haste to a Judean town in the hill country, where she entered the house of Zechariah and greeted Elizabeth. When Elizabeth heard Mary's greeting, the child leaped in her womb. And Elizabeth was filled with the Holy Spirit and exclaimed with a loud cry, "Blessed are you among women, and blessed is the fruit of your womb. And why has this happened to me, that the mother of my Lord comes to me? For as soon as I heard the sound of your greeting, the child in my womb leaped for joy. And blessed is she who believed that there would be a fulfillment of what was spoken to her by the Lord."*

To contemplate:

Mary, now a virgin mother,
    carries in her womb the one
who gladdens his great herald-to-be,
    the infant in her cousin's womb.

Elizabeth knows what is taking place,
    knows by the Spirit's inner voice
Mary is not just another mother;
    her son is not just another child:

"Blest are you among all women,
  and blest is your most holy child!
Who am I that God's chosen mother
  brings my Lord himself to me?
Yes, dear Mary, most blest are you
  for having believed in the word of God,
believed his word by angel's voice:
  he sends his Son to be your child!"

O Mary, for your most loving faith
  God chose you to mother his own Son,
blest are you among all women,
  the one who really loved the most—
loved enough to serve your God
  as his own humble virgin maid,
though all the world might call disgrace
  such faithful service to the Lord!

Come to me as you came to John,
  to bless my infant inner life.
Bring me your child to anoint my soul,
  and Holy Spirit to dwell in me.
And I, like John, will leap for joy,
  and believe with the love
  with which you believe!

Mary's Song of Gratitude to God

Lk 1:46-49:

And Mary said,
"My soul magnifies the Lord,
and my spirit rejoices in God my Savior,
for he has looked with favor
on the lowliness
of his servant.
Surely, from now on
all generations will call me blessed;
for the Mighty One
has done great things for me,
and holy is his name."

To contemplate:

Your prayer, dear Mary,
tells us why God chose you,
among all the women he created,
to mother his own dear Son.
Your loving prayer of praise
reveals your heart; so humble,
it exists only to magnify
the God you serve.

We can look through you,
God's small magnifying glass,
to glimpse the greatness
of the Lord who made
of his little handmaid
the greatest mother
of the greatest child
of all the ages!

Thus, every time
we call you "Blessed,"
we call God "Holy."
Every time we praise you, Mary,
we praise God more.

With Gabriel and Elizabeth, then, we pray:
"Hail Mary, full of grace,
the Lord is with you;
blessed are you among women,
and blessed is the fruit of your womb, Jesus!"

Mary's Love for God's Mercy

Lk 1:50-56:

"His mercy is for those who fear him
from generation to generation.
He has shown strength with his arm;
he has scattered the proud
in the thoughts of their hearts.
He has brought down the powerful from their thrones,
and lifted up the lowly;
he has filled the hungry with good things,
and sent the rich away empty.
He has helped his servant Israel,
in remembrance of his mercy,
according to the promise he made to our ancestors,
to Abraham and to his descendants forever."
And Mary remained with her about three months
and then returned to her home.

To contemplate:

Your God, dear Mary,
is the God of absolute mercy
for those who adore only him,
absolute justice for those who exalt themselves.

The proud of heart who flaunt their power
to gather riches for themselves
and scorn the poor—
these your God scatters like dead leaves.

But the lowly and the poor,
who know they need him,
he raises up and gives good things.
For his chosen people
he now fulfills his promise of mercy—
his promise of his Anointed One
to save us from our sins.

Ah, Mary,
that promise is now fulfilled
in you.
You carry in your womb your son—
God's Son who has come
to save the world.
Bring him to us, too,
sweet Mary!

The Birth of John the Baptist

Lk 1:57-79: *Now the time came for Elizabeth to give birth, and she bore a son.... On the eighth day they came to circumcise the child.... And [Zechariah] wrote, "His name is John."...*

Then his father Zechariah was filled with the Holy Spirit and spoke this prophecy:
"Blessed be the Lord God of Israel,
for he has looked favorably on his people
and redeemed them.
He has raised up a mighty savior for us
in the house of his servant David,
as he spoke through the mouth
of his holy prophets from of old....
And you, child, will be called
the prophet of the Most High;
for you will go before the Lord to prepare his ways,
to give knowledge of salvation to his people
by the forgiveness of their sins.
By the tender mercy of our God,
the dawn from on high will break upon us,
to give light to those who sit in darkness
and in the shadow of death,
to guide our feet into the way of peace."

To contemplate:

Ah, Zechariah, at last you speak,
now that you've obeyed the angel's word
to call your son "John,"
this name means "Yahweh has shown favor."
For out of the darkness that covers us,
out of the hollowness of night,
Yahweh's dawn will burst as the brightest light
the world has ever seen!

Not only does John now live,
so does the Savior he will herald—
David's heir, whom Mary bears,
foretold by prophets long ago.

God's favor—his own Son—
is the dawn of our new life,
the light brighter than our sun
breaking up death's black abyss.

John, like day-star presaging sun,
will prepare weak eyes for the greater light
that illumines the way to eternal life.

O Lord of light, break up my gloom!

Jesus Enters Our Race

Lk 2:1-7: *In those days a decree went out from Emperor Augustus that all the world should be registered.... All went to their own towns to be registered. Joseph also went from the town of Nazareth in Galilee to Judea, to the city of David called Bethlehem, because he was descended from the house and family of David. He went to be registered with Mary, to whom he was engaged and who was expecting a child. While they were there, the time came for her to deliver her child. And she gave birth to her firstborn son and wrapped him in bands of cloth, and laid him in a manger, because there was no place for them in the inn.*

To contemplate:

Into the history of the Roman realm
    enters the Lord of all the world.
Caesar Augustus gives command,
    and the Lord of the world obeys!
Of David's royal stock is he;
    yet he obeys the petty whim
of a proud ruler who takes the count
    of ancient peoples he commands.

Through Joseph, faithful foster father,
   and Mary, sweetest loving mother,
the unborn infant obeys the king
   who counts him with the rest.

The worldly kings make noxious noise
   to have their will, their petty way.
But the king of heaven comes silently
   into this suffering world of sin.
Humble stable, a home for him,
   animal feeding-trough for bed,
and bands of cloth against the cold—
   nothing more for him.
No room in the inn, no place for him;
   the poor of this world are richer far
than the child from heaven who comes to them—
   child who will save from sin.
Ignored, abandoned by all the world,
   in darkest silence of night comes he,
as though ashamed to lay firm claim
   to the glory that is his.

O infant Jesus, defenseless babe,
   with mother Mary and Joseph brave,
I kneel before your sleeping face,
   adoring silently....

Good News of Great Joy
for All the People

Lk 2:8-14: *In that region there were shepherds living in the fields, keeping watch over their flock by night. Then an angel of the Lord stood before them, and the glory of the Lord shone around them, and they were terrified. But the angel said to them, "Do not be afraid; for see—I am bringing you good news of great joy for all the people: to you is born this day in the city of David a Savior, who is the Messiah, the Lord. This will be a sign for you: you will find a child wrapped in bands of cloth and lying in a manger." And suddenly there was with the angel a multitude of the heavenly host, praising God and saying, "Glory to God in the highest heaven, and on earth peace among those whom he favors!"*

To contemplate:

Into deep silence of the night
   bursts the angels' song,
a song of joy only shepherds hear—
   simple folk know angels sing.
Like Mary's song, the angels' song
   tells the best of news,

news of the birth of the promised prince—
    the world's anointed child,
the child who is the glory of God,
    Lord of the highest heaven;
the child who is the peace of earth,
    peace of all men and women.

God's angels know the deepest sense
    of the event that they announce;
to his greatest glory God gives to us
    the choicest of his favors:
the child who himself will shepherd us
    and bring us home to God,
has come at last in simple guise,
    as humblest of us all!
The humble one who comes to us
    is hailed by humble folk;
the rich ignore him, know him not,
    in their utter emptiness.

O humble Lord of all the world,
    lowly Messiah Lord,
O Savior of all who hear the song
    of angels on the wind,

come to us, too, and in our lives
    fulfill the angels' song!

Mary Treasures
the Shepherds' Words

Lk 2:15-20: *When the angels had left them and gone into heaven, the shepherds said to one another, "Let us go now to Bethlehem and see this thing that has taken place, which the Lord has made known to us." So they went with haste and found Mary and Joseph, and the child lying in the manger. When they saw this, they made known what had been told them about this child; and all who heard it were amazed at what the shepherds told them. But Mary treasured all these words and pondered them in her heart. The shepherds returned, glorifying and praising God for all they had heard and seen, as it had been told them.*

To contemplate:

Only the poor can find the child;
   only the poor can know
the secret of God, his hidden way—
   the secret of his Son.
Like any child, he lies so still,
   a newborn in a manger;
he cries like any other child—
   a stranger in strange world.

No sign he gives of special gift,
　　no glint in knowing eye.
Yet shepherds acknowledge the secret truth
　　of the angels' secret song.
They tell their tale, a fairy tale
　　to the wealthy of this world,
but an angel tale of greatest news
　　to the poor who hear God's word.

They tell their tale and those who hear
　　are amazed at such good news.
But there is one who really hears
　　and treasures in her heart
the angels' glorious song of joy.

She ponders to its greatest depth
　　its meaning for her life.
Daily, hourly, she meditates
　　the angels' song of joy,
as she contemplates her child.

O Mary, teach us how to hear
　　the very voice of God
in such small incidents of life
　　as visit of shepherds poor,
who speak God's truth about your child.

Mary and Joseph Keep the Law

Lk 2:21-24: *After eight days had passed, it was time to circumcise the child; and he was called Jesus, the name given by the angel before he was conceived in the womb.*

When the time came for their purification according to the law of Moses, they brought him up to Jerusalem to present him to the Lord (as it is written in the law of the Lord, "Every firstborn male shall be designated as holy to the Lord"), and they offered a sacrifice according to what is stated in the law of the Lord, "a pair of turtle-doves or two young pigeons."

To contemplate:

Jesus enters his Father's people,
    wounded in circumcision,
tiny preview of his cross
    to fulfill God's covenant.
And in accord with Gabriel's word,
    he's named after Joshua,
for he will lead his people forth
    into God's promised land.

His holy parents fulfill the law
   of Mary's purification—
the purest of all virgins pure
   is legally purified.
And Jesus, like any firstborn son,
   is presented in the temple—
the holy Son of God himself
   fulfills God's law for men.
Instead of a lamb they offer up
   two doves, in poverty.
The richest people in God's grace
   are poor in earthly goods.

O Joseph, righteous man of faith,
   help us obey God's law,
the law that comes to us through men,
   and yet fulfills God's will.
O Mary, purest of holy women,
   teach us your purity—
obedient to the will of God,
   no matter what the cost.

O Jesus, Son of God most high,
   grace us to follow you,
up steepest temple steps of life,
   to give ourselves to God!

Simeon's Prophecy

Lk 2:25-32: *Now there was a man in Jerusalem whose name was Simeon; this man was righteous and devout, looking forward to the consolation of Israel, and the Holy Spirit rested on him. It had been revealed to him by the Holy Spirit that he would not see death before he had seen the Lord's Messiah. Guided by the Spirit, Simeon came into the temple; and when the parents brought in the child Jesus, to do for him what was customary under the law, Simeon took him in his arms and praised God, saying,*

> *"Master, now you are dismissing*
>   *your servant in peace, according to your word;*
> *for my eyes have seen your salvation,*
>   *which you have prepared in the presence*
>   *of all peoples,*
> *a light for revelation to the Gentiles*
>   *and for glory to your people Israel."*

To contemplate:

God's ancient servant Simeon
  sees in Mary's infant son
    the promise he's been waiting for.

The Spirit guides him to the temple,
    the Spirit who promised he would see
        the Savior whom God would send the world.
The Spirit reveals Mary's child;
    Simeon takes him in his arms,
        his soul enwrapped in God's own peace.
His arms now hold the world's salvation:
    the glory of his people Israel,
        the revelation to the Gentiles.
Here is God's Son for all the world,
    hope of all who droop in darkness,
        glory of all who seek the light.

Infant, I too would hold you tight,
    hold you close to beating heart,
        touch you with my trembling hands.
What joy to let your little fingers
    entwine my own in grip of might,
        your tiny feet press on my chest.

What joy, my Lord, to hear your voice
    gurgle the joy of human life,
        as I whisper in your tiny ear.
What joy to gaze into your eyes,
    explore eternal depths in pools
        where Spirit dwells in love divine!

Jesus Grows in Wisdom and Favor

Lk 2:33-40: *And the child's father and mother were amazed at what was being said about him. Then Simeon blessed them and said to his mother Mary, "This child is destined for the falling and the rising of many in Israel, and to be a sign that will be opposed so that the inner thoughts of many will be revealed—and a sword will pierce your own soul too."*

There was also a prophet, Anna the daughter of Phanuel, of the tribe of Asher. She was of a great age, having lived with her husband seven years after her marriage, then as a widow to the age of eighty-four. She never left the temple but worshiped there with fasting and prayer night and day. At that moment she came, and began to praise God and to speak about the child to all who were looking for the redemption of Jerusalem.

When they had finished everything required by the law of the Lord, they returned to Galilee, to their own town of Nazareth. The child grew and became strong, filled with wisdom; and the favor of God was upon him.

To contemplate:

This child is history's great divide:
    he separates the good from bad,
sorts out the secret thoughts of all—
    thoughts of love from thoughts of hate.
He'll suffer nail-pierced hands and feet,
    while his mother suffers sword-pierced soul.
He'll hang upon his bloodied cross
    to reveal God's love for us!

O Mary, help him bear his pain—
    the pain of peer-rejected child,
the pain of growing into a man
    who foresees his road of sacrifice.
A word for you to treasure now:
    not angel's word but prophet's word
to deliberate through all the days
    of watching child grow into man.

Another word from prophetess:
    more cheerful word of aged Anna,
word of praise for the holy child
    who will redeem Jerusalem.
Then back to Nazareth in Galilee,
    to ponder these words year by year,
and watch him grow up strong and wise
    in the daily presence of your God.

O Mary, treasurer of all *his* words,
    guard them here within my heart!

The Boy Jesus in the Temple

Lk 2:41-47: *Now every year his parents went to Jerusalem for the festival of the Passover. And when he was twelve years old, they went up as usual for the festival. When the festival was ended and they started to return, the boy Jesus stayed behind in Jerusalem, but his parents did not know it. Assuming that he was in the group of travelers, they went a day's journey. Then they started to look for him among their relatives and friends. When they did not find him, they returned to Jerusalem to search for him. After three days they found him in the temple, sitting among the teachers, listening to them and asking them questions. And all who heard him were amazed at his understanding and his answers.*

To contemplate:

Twelve mysterious years fly by,
   twelve years of sun and shadow.
O Lord, the silence of those years—
   what did they hold for you?
Did Joseph teach you carpentry?
   Did Mary tell you stories?

Did you play with other boys
    and sit in school with them?

O Luke, why are you silent here?
    Could you find naught to tell—
only that he grew strong and wise,
    like any other child?

Then, as a Jewish boy of twelve,
    he goes up to Jerusalem.
But unlike other boys of twelve,
    he's lost in temple praise,
then sits among the teachers sage,
    absorbing every word,
asking questions they fathom not—
    he's wiser than them all!
They find his answers too profound;
    they marvel at his depth
and wonder who he really is,
    this simple boy of twelve.

O Jesus, when you were a boy,
    did you play like other boys?
Did you laugh and sing and run and dance—
    and kneel to pray and dream?
O Mary, how you embraced and held
    his words within your heart!

"I Must Be in My Father's House"

Lk 2:48-52: *When his parents saw him they were astonished; and his mother said to him, "Child, why have you treated us like this? Look, your father and I have been searching for you in great anxiety." He said to them, "Why were you searching for me? Did you not know that I must be in my Father's house?" But they did not understand what he said to them. Then he went down with them and came to Nazareth, and was obedient to them. His mother treasured all these things in her heart.*

And Jesus increased in wisdom and in years, and in divine and human favor.

To contemplate:

His parents are astonished, too,
    but not because he's wise.
They're surprised he stayed behind,
    causing them such grief.
Mary, like mothers everywhere,
    requires an explanation,
baring to him the inner hurt
    of days of seeking him.

He reveals to them his own surprise
    they have not yet perceived
that now he really does belong
    within his Father's house.

What is that he says to them,
    "I must be in my Father's house"?
How can he call God's great temple
    simply his Father's house?
What arrogance in a boy of twelve,
    to call God his own Father
and the temple his Father's house!
    Who does he think he is?
No less than God's one only Son,
    no less than the Son of God!
Yet they scold him not nor reprimand,
    though they do not understand.

Then home with them to Nazareth,
    obedient as before.
His mother treasures these new words
    deep within her heart.
O Mary, help me find in him
    the boy who won your heart,
O Jesus, Mary's son and God's,
    mature in my poor heart!

Lk 3:1-20 = Mt 3:1-12 ("=" is used here to indicate approximately
parallel passages, presented in Matthew: Our Healing God-With-
Us_): John the Baptist's proclamation._

The
Public Ministry
of **Jesus**

The Baptism of Jesus

Lk 3:21-22: *Now when all the people were baptized, and when Jesus also had been baptized and was praying, the heaven was opened, and the Holy Spirit descended upon him in bodily form like a dove. And a voice came from heaven, "You are my Son, the Beloved; with you I am well pleased."*

To contemplate:

Jesus prays as no one else has prayed,
   a prayer so perfect
      the Dove of peace,
       the Spirit-Dove,
         now rests on him.
And the almighty everlasting God
   speaks out to him—
      not in thunder
        as at Sinai (cf. Ex 19:19)—
          but in paternal love:

"You are my Son, my own beloved Son;
    with you I am well pleased.
        When you were twelve,
            you called me 'Father';
                I've always called you 'Son!'"
Sight and sound combine to tell us
    who you are, my Lord:
        the Prince of Peace—
            of Holy-Spirit Peace,
                of loving-Father Peace!
O Prince, I pray to you for peace,
    peace of inner spirit,
        soul-peace, dove-peace,
            pervading all my thoughts,
                desires and acts.
O Son of God, Father-beloved,
    I pray to be with you
        the Father's only Son—
            to call him "My Father,"
                hear him say "My son!"
O Father, Son and Holy Spirit,
    I, too, was baptized
        in your triune life;
            I, too, am a person of peace;
                I, too, am a child of God!

Jesus' Family Tree

Lk 3:23-38: *Jesus was about thirty years old when he began his work. He was the son (as was thought) of Joseph son of Heli, son of Matthat...son of David...son of Jacob, son of Isaac, son of Abraham...son of Adam, son of God.*

To contemplate:

Names, many names of ancient forebears—
  a family tree by Luke;
    a list unlike
      Matthew's list
        from David on.
Matthew lists a line of kings from David
  down to Israel's exile;
    Luke's list
      up to David
        is much humbler.
Who gives us Jesus' family line exact—
  Matthew or Luke?
    Do they care,
      except to say,
        "He's one of us"?

One thing is sure to both of them:
    Jesus is a member
        of our race,
            firmly in line
                from Abraham.
And not only Abraham, says Luke,
    but back to Adam
        and even God.
            Jesus is made
                in God's image.
Luke has just identified his Jesus
    as Prince of Peace
        and Son of God;
            yet he's also man,
                as human as we.
O Jesus, Prince of Peace and Son of God!
    man like me,
        mysteriously
            hiding divinity
            in humanity.
O Jesus, Person of the Trinity,
    I adore and love you—
        man like me!

Lk 4:1-13 = Mt 4:1-11 The temptation of Jesus in the wilderness.

Jesus, God's Anointed One

Lk 4:14-21: *Then Jesus, filled with the power of the Spirit, returned to Galilee, and a report about him spread through all the surrounding country. He began to teach in their synagogues and was praised by everyone. When he came to Nazareth, where he had been brought up, he went to the synagogue on the sabbath day, as was his custom. He stood up to read, and the scroll of the prophet Isaiah was given to him. He unrolled the scroll and found the place where it was written:*

> *"The Spirit of the Lord is upon me,*
> > *because he has anointed me*
> > *to bring good news to the poor.*
> *He has sent me to proclaim release to the captives*
> > *and recovery of sight to the blind,*
> > *to let the oppressed go free,*
> > *to proclaim the year of the Lord's favor."*

And he rolled up the scroll, gave it back to the attendant, and sat down. The eyes of all in the synagogue were fixed on him. Then he began to say to them, "Today this scripture has been fulfilled in your hearing."

To contemplate:

All eyes are firmly fixed on him,
  sensing a moment of truth.
Filled with the Holy Spirit's power,
  he reveals God's secret plan.
He reads the promise of Isaiah,
  prophet of long ago—
the promise of God's Anointed One
  he now proclaims fulfilled,
fulfilled in him the one they see,
  the man who speaks to them.
They stare in shock of disbelief:
  How could he say such thing?
Could he be the Spirit-anointed one,
  the long-awaited herald
sent by God to bring good news
  to the poor, the slave, the blind?
Is this the time of greatest favor,
  the true year of the Lord,
when all debts are indeed forgiven,
  all our wrongs made right?
O Jesus Christ, Anointed One,
  I believe you are God's voice!
O Jesus, Lord, I welcome you,
  for I am poor and blind.

Jesus' Rejection at Nazareth

Lk 4:24-30: *And he said, "Truly I tell you, no prophet is accepted in the prophet's hometown. But the truth is, there were many widows in Israel in the time of Elijah, when the heaven was shut up three years and six months, and there was a severe famine over all the land; yet Elijah was sent to none of them except to a widow at Zarephath in Sidon. There were also many lepers in Israel in the time of the prophet Elisha, and none of them was cleansed except Naaman the Syrian." When they heard this, all in the synagogue were filled with rage. They got up, drove him out of the town, and led him to the brow of the hill on which their town was built, so that they might hurl him off the cliff. But he passed through the midst of them and went on his way.*

To contemplate:

They hear him say Isaiah's word
   has been fulfilled in him.
It is a thought so strange to them,
   they do not comprehend.

At first they marvel at his speech,
  so gracious are his words.
But when they fall to earth at last,
  he's only one of them—
the son of Joseph they had known
  as lowly carpenter.
How can the son of Joseph know
  so much more than they?
How can he presume to teach,
  unlearned as he is?
No rabbi, he; they know him well
  as simply Joseph's son.

So they begin to turn from him;
  he tries to win them back.
He knows the truth about himself:
  a prophet as no other,
but as they often have been spurned,
  so will it be with him.
They drove him from their meeting place
  to throw him off a cliff!

O Jesus, truest of all prophets—
  I do believe in you!

Lk 4:31-44 = Mk 1:21-39 (see Mark: A Very Human Jesus*): Jesus releases a man from an unclean spirit.*

Jesus Catches Simon Peter

Lk 5:1-11: Once while Jesus was standing beside the lake of Gennesaret, and the crowd was pressing in on him to hear the word of God, he saw two boats there at the shore of the lake.... He got into one of the boats, the one belonging to Simon, and asked him to put out a little way from the shore. Then he sat down and taught the crowds from the boat. When he had finished speaking, he said to Simon, "Put out into the deep water and let down your nets for a catch." Simon answered, "Master, we have worked all night long but have caught nothing. Yet if you say so, I will let down the nets." When they had done this, they caught so many fish that their nets were beginning to break. So they signaled their partners in the other boat to come and help them. And they came and filled both boats, so that they began to sink. But when Simon Peter saw it, he fell down at Jesus' knees, saying, "Go away from me, Lord, for I am a sinful man!" For he and all who were with him were amazed at the catch of fish that they had taken; and so also were James and John, sons of Zebedee, who were partners with Simon. Then Jesus said to Simon, "Do not be afraid; from now on you will be catching people." When they had brought their boats to shore, they left everything and followed him.

To contemplate:

A story to delight the heart of any fisherman—
the fisherman himself is caught!
Simon knows this lake,
knows the fish might bite at night,
but if they don't, they surely won't by day.
Yet Jesus knows the man he's out to catch,
knows the sins that sadden him,
his heart abhorring them,
his readiness to see the light,
humility to take advice he thinks off course.

Jesus works a miracle this man can understand,
a catch enough to sink his boat.
Shaken, Simon sinks,
confessing his unworthiness
in the presence of the man who does such things.
Before he can be Peter, he must know
he is naught without his Lord.
Jesus accepts remorse,
lifts Simon up to make him rock,
leader of those he'll make his fishermen!

O Jesus, great fisherman of all the world,
catch me, poor person of many sins—
send me to fish for you!

---

*Lk 5:12-6:16 = Mk 1:40-3:19 Jesus cures a leper and a paralytic, calls
Levi, answers questions about fasting and the sabbath, cures a man
with a withered hand, and chooses his twelve apostles.*

Jesus Heals Them All

Lk 6:17-23: *He came down with them and stood on a level place, with a great crowd of his disciples and a great multitude of people from all Judea, Jerusalem, and the coast of Tyre and Sidon. They had come to hear him and to be healed of their diseases; and those who were troubled with unclean spirits were cured. And all in the crowd were trying to touch him, for power came out from him and healed all of them.*

To contemplate:

Here is the man the Spirit anointed
    to drive out unclean spirits;
This is the Son that God has sent
    to heal his other children.
They come to him from far and near,
    driven by new white hope
and a vague faith that this carpenter
    can mend bodies and spirits.
The crippled, the maimed, the wasting away
    come limping, crawling to him.

He stoops to lift them one by one
    from the dust to the clearing air.
The broken-hearted from distant lands
    are carried in hope to him.
He touches hearts with his own meek heart
    and once more they see the sky.
Men with tormented, twisted minds
    find their way to him.
He lays his hands upon their heads
    and their demons pass away.
Has ever a man so served all others?
    Has ever a love like this
won the hearts and minds of all—
    the poor and broken-hearted?

O Jesus, I, too, come to you—
    afflicted as I am,
I touch your loving, sacred heart
    in faith and hope and love.
Oh, stoop to me, lift up my head,
    that I may face the world,
trusting that you will comfort me
    and heal me in your love.

Jesus Teaches the Way to Joy

Lk 6:20-26: *Then he looked up at his disciples and said:*
"Blessed are you who are poor,
for yours is the kingdom of God.
"Blessed are you who are hungry now,
for you will be filled.
"Blessed are you who weep now,
for you will laugh.

"Blessed are you when people hate you, and when they exclude you, revile you, and defame you on account of the Son of Man. Rejoice in that day and leap for joy, for surely your reward is great in heaven; for that is what their ancestors did to the prophets.

"But woe to you who are rich,
for you have received your consolation.
"Woe to you who are full now,
for you will be hungry.
"Woe to you who are laughing now,
for you will mourn and weep.
"Woe to you when all speak well of you,
for that is what their ancestors did to the false prophets."

To contemplate:

Four blessings for bearing hate and pain;
 four warnings against evasion.
Those who seek their riches now,
 or strive to fill each want,
to find their joy in things of earth,
 and worldly reputation—
these will find but emptiness,
 theirs, no consolation,
no lasting happiness or joy,
 no satisfying peace.
The Wisdom who accompanied God
 in the making of the world
now speaks his word of wisdom deep
 to all who want to live:

"Don't worry if you're poor and hungry;
 then you are truly blest,
for yours will be the kingdom of God,
 where you will have your rest.
When you must weep for being scorned,
 remember I suffered thus;
with me you'll laugh and leap for joy
 in a kingdom God made for us!"

Lk 6:27-31 = Mt 5:38-44 Jesus demands that we love even our enemies.

Be Merciful As
Your Father Is Merciful

Lk 6:32-36: *"If you love those who love you, what credit is that to you? For even sinners love those who love them. If you do good to those who do good to you, what credit is that to you? For even sinners do the same. If you lend to those from whom you hope to receive, what credit is that to you? Even sinners lend to sinners, to receive as much again. But love your enemies, do good, and lend, expecting nothing in return. Your reward will be great, and you will be children of the Most High; for he is kind to the ungrateful and the wicked. Be merciful, just as your Father is merciful."*

To contemplate:

The God of Jesus is a different God
    from the gods of Greece and Rome;
the God of Jesus is a unique God
    beyond all human ken.
What other God is merciful
    to the hateful and the base?
But who wants a God compassionate
    to the undeserving vile?

Give us a God of equity,
    who richly rewards the good
and sternly castigates the bad—
we want a righteous God!

Yet, what would he not find in us?
    Do we not lend for profit?
Do we help those who will disdain
    to thank us for our care?
Do we show mercy to the cruel,
    compassion to the callous,
forgiveness to the unforgiving,
    and kindness to the unkind?
By Jesus' standard we still lack
    the mercy of our God.
Next to his goodness absolute
    our "goodness" is most vile.

O Jesus, you show our Father's mercy
    in all your words and acts!
Yet I cannot love my enemies
    unless you love in me.
O my compassionate Father-God,
    make me your child of mercy
    in the mercy of your Son!

Lk 6:37-49 = Mt 7:1-27 Jesus forbids us to judge others.
Lk 7:1-10 = Mt 8:5-13 Jesus heals a centurion's servant.

Jesus Restores a Dead Son to Life

Lk 7:11-17: *Soon afterwards he went to a town called Nain, and his disciples and a large crowd went with him. As he approached the gate of the town, a man who had died was being carried out. He was his mother's only son, and she was a widow; and with her was a large crowd from the town. When the Lord saw her, he had compassion for her and said to her, "Do not weep." Then he came forward and touched the bier, and the bearers stood still. And he said, "Young man, I say to you, rise!" The dead man sat up and began to speak, and Jesus gave him to his mother. Fear seized all of them; and they glorified God, saying, "A great prophet has risen among us!" and "God has looked favorably on his people!" This word about him spread throughout Judea and all the surrounding country.*

To contemplate:

A scene of grief: a widow mourns
   the death of her only son
     as they carry him
     to bury him.

Jesus comes upon the scene
    and grieves along with her;
        he cannot bear
        her grieving tear.
What will he do, just weep with her
    and pass on down the street?
        What can he do—
        the man is dead!
First, he comforts the weeping widow;
    he lovingly shares her grief,
        compassionately says:
        "Do not weep."

Then he turns to the work at hand:
    he halts the funeral's course
        and addresses
        the dead man:
"Young man, I say to you, rise up!"
    He restores him to his mother,
        compassionately,
        lovingly.

Lord, see the tears of Mother Mary
    for her poor dying children—
        raise us up
        to follow her!

Lk 7:18-35 = Mt 11:2-19 Jesus praises John the Baptist.

Jesus Pardons a Sinful Woman

Lk 7:36-50: *One of the Pharisees asked Jesus to eat with him.... And a woman in the city, who was a sinner...brought an alabaster jar of ointment. She stood behind him at his feet, weeping, and began to bathe his feet with her tears and to dry them with her hair. Then she continued kissing his feet and anointing them with the ointment. Now when the Pharisee who had invited him saw it, he said to himself, "If this man were a prophet, he would have known who and what kind of woman this is who is touching him—that she is a sinner." Jesus spoke up and said to him.... "A certain creditor had two debtors; one owed five hundred denarii, and the other fifty. When they could not pay, he canceled the debts for both of them. Now which of them will love him more?" Simon answered, "I suppose the one for whom he canceled the greater debt." And Jesus said to him, "You have judged rightly.... I entered your house; you gave me no water for my feet, but she has bathed my feet with her tears and dried them with her hair. You gave me no kiss, but...she has not stopped kissing my feet. You did not anoint my head with oil, but she has anointed my feet with ointment. Therefore, I tell you, her sins, which were many, have been forgiven; hence she has shown*

great love. But the one to whom little is forgiven, loves little." Then he said to her, "Your sins are forgiven." But those who were at the table with him began to say among themselves, "Who is this who even forgives sins?" And he said to the woman, "Your faith has saved you; go in peace."

To contemplate:

Intuitively, this woman knows he will forgive—
    is already pardoning her many sins!
There's something in his face that tells her this,
    something Simon never sees.

As great her sins before he came into her life,
    so great is now her overflowing love.
As costly as her sins have been to her and hers,
    so precious now her tears.

To her tears she adds an alabaster jar of ointment,
    in humility that is not humiliating;
for his gentle reception of her tender service
    blanks out all hostile stares.

Will Simon learn the lesson of her humility?
    Can he turn his admiration into love?
Will the question of his other guests
    stir his sorrow for his sins?

O dear, compassionate Lord, forgiver of all sins,
    forgive the sins I lay before your feet
        with the ointment of my tears.

Women Also Follow Jesus

Lk 8:1-3: *Soon afterward he went on through cities and villages, proclaiming and bringing the good news of the kingdom of God. The twelve were with him, as well as some women who had been cured of evil spirits and infirmities: Mary, called Magdalene, from whom seven demons had gone out, and Joanna, the wife of Herod's steward Chuza, and Susanna, and many others, who provided for them out of their resources.*

To contemplate:

Luke's saving Lord is fully man,
    a man who loves all women—
but not in the narrow sense of "love"
    our world equates with lust.
He loves the woman in Simon's house
    and the women following him,
accepts their minist'ring to his needs,
    their providing for the twelve.
They furnish whatever his men forget
    or neglect in a careless way.

They take care of daily details
    in a loving and caring way.
Some he's released from the tyranny
    of Satan and his horde;
some have come from such high estate,
    as Herod's royal court.
But all are welcome to come to him
    and serve him in his needs.
These women serve the Minister
    of all our deep desires.
They're with him all along his way
    through ancient Galilee;
they'll be with him on his final walk,
    his journey to Jerusalem.
They'll be with him even on Calvary,
    help take him from his cross;
they'll lay him in good Joseph's tomb
    and return on Easter morn.

More faithful than the men are they;
    more loving and caring, too,
like faithful women down the years,
    caring for careless men.

O Lord, we men thank you most gratefully
    for your gift of womankind!

Lk 8:4-18 = Mk 4:1-25 *The parables of the sower and of the lamp.*

Jesus' Mother Heeds God's Word

Lk 8:19-21: *Then his mother and his brothers came to him, but they could not reach him because of the crowd. And he was told, "Your mother and your brothers are standing outside, wanting to see you." But he said to them, "My mother and my brothers are those who hear the word of God and do it."*

To contemplate:

Who was first in your Gospel, Luke,
   to hear and do God's word?
Not Zechariah, John's priestly father;
   he doubted Gabriel's pledge.
Mary was first to believe his word,
   and truly first to say:
"I am the servant of the Lord;
   I embrace his holy word!"
And Mary was the first to greet
   with the Savior in her womb
Elizabeth and her unborn son,
   John, the future Baptist.

And Mary magnified the Lord
    in prayerful, holy song,
extolling his magnanimous mercy
    to the poorest of the poor.
Then Mary gave birth to God's own Son
    in distant Bethlehem;
she held him in her virgin arms,
    cared for and nurtured him.
It was Mary who believed the song
    of angels to the shepherds
and treasured all the words they spoke
    in her purest of pure hearts.
With Joseph she took him to the temple
    and offered him to God.
With Joseph she found him in the temple
    teaching his Father's word.
Now, Luke, your Jesus tells us clear
    we must become like her,
if we'd become his dearest kin—
    we must hear and heed God's word.

Sweet Mary, mother of my Lord,
teach me to do as you have done—
    bring forth his word in me.

_____

Lk 8:22-56 = Mk 4:35-5:43 Jesus calms a storm, heals the Gerasene demoniac, the woman suffering from hemorrhages, and restores a girl to life.

Who Is This Man?

Lk 9:1-9: *Then Jesus called the twelve together and gave them power and authority over all demons and to cure diseases, and he sent them out to proclaim the kingdom of God and to heal. He said to them, "Take nothing for your journey, no staff, nor bag, nor bread, nor money— not even an extra tunic. Whatever house you enter, stay there, and leave from there. Wherever they do not welcome you, as you are leaving that town shake the dust off your feet as a testimony against them." They departed and went through the villages, bringing the good news and curing diseases everywhere.*

Now Herod the ruler heard about all that had taken place, and he was perplexed, because it was said by some that John had been raised from the dead, by some that Elijah had appeared, and by others that one of the ancient prophets had arisen. Herod said, "John I beheaded; but who is this about whom I hear such things?" And he tried to see him.

To contemplate:

Poor Herod thought his troubles gone
    when he cut off the Baptist's head.
But now another preacher's come,
    more popular than John.
Could this new one be the old returned,
    or perhaps the great Elijah,
or ancient prophet risen up?
    Whoever he is, look out!
He's trouble for a king like Herod;
    his good news to the weak and poor
will be bad news to an evil king!
    Who is this good-news man?

Luke suggests some credible clues:
    Jesus empowers men
to fight with demons and prevail
    with his incredible news;
he will now begin to feed his people
    with scarce supply of food—
feed five thousand men with five small loaves
    and no more than two small fish!
He feeds their minds with strange new truths,
    their bodies with miraculous food.
No wonder Herod is deeply moved.
    Can a ruler permit such things?

O Jesus, you are a dangerous man
    to rulers in Herod's mold!

Peter Recognizes Jesus
As the Messiah

Lk 9:18-23: *Once when Jesus was praying alone, with only the disciples near him, he asked them, "Who do the crowds say that I am?" They answered, "John the Baptist; but others, Elijah; and still others, that one of the ancient prophets has arisen." He said to them, "But who do you say that I am?" Peter answered, "The Messiah of God."*

He sternly ordered and commanded them not to tell anyone, saying, "The Son of Man must undergo great suffering, and be rejected by the elders, chief priests, and scribes, and be killed, and on the third day be raised."

Then he said to them all, "If any want to become my followers, let them deny themselves and take up their cross daily and follow me."

To contemplate:

Herod's question, "Who is this?"
　　is also on other minds.
Jesus departs from the crowd to pray
　　and question his disciples.
First he asks them about the crowds;
　　their answers are like Herod's.

When he puts the question straight to them,
    Peter answers for them all:
"You are the Messiah of God, the Christ!"
    Ah, Peter, you answer well—
much better than Herod or the crowd,
    much better than you think.

You've heard his words and seen his acts—
    you know he's sent by God.
But do you know the deeper sense
    of that phrase "Messiah of God"—
that it will include more suffering
    than you have ever dreamt?
Do you know that he will be maligned,
    and even put to death?
Do you know that if you walk with him,
    you must deny yourself,
take up your cross and follow him,
    daily—till your death?

O Peter, you will follow him,
    and die even as he died—
        crucified!
O Peter, please now pray for us,
    that, like you, we too
        follow him!

Lk 9:24-27 = Mk 8:34-9:1 "Those who want to save their life will lose it."

Jesus Prepares His Exodus

Lk 9:28-36: *Now about eight days after these sayings Jesus took with him Peter and John and James, and went up on the mountain to pray. And while he was praying, the appearance of his face changed, and his clothes became dazzling white. Suddenly they saw two men, Moses and Elijah, talking to him. They appeared in glory and were speaking of his departure, which he was about to accomplish at Jerusalem. Now Peter and his companions were weighed down with sleep; but since they had stayed awake, they saw his glory and the two men who stood with him. Just as they were leaving him, Peter said to Jesus, "Master, it is good for us to be here; let us make three dwellings, one for you, one for Moses, and one for Elijah"—not knowing what he said. While he was saying this, a cloud came and overshadowed them; and they were terrified as they entered the cloud. Then from the cloud came a voice that said, "This is my Son, my Chosen; listen to him!" When the voice had spoken, Jesus was found alone. And they kept silent and in those days told no one any of the things they had seen.*

To contemplate:

Jesus' glory flashes through his prayer,
  radiates through his human features
    the glory of the Lord!
Till now he's hid transcendent divinity,
  but it is time to brace his men
    to bear the coming trials.

He talks with ancient Moses and Elijah—
  with Moses, leader of the Exodus,
    and Elijah of chariot fame.
They speak of his own approaching exodus
  from his people in Jerusalem—
    his exodus in death!

Moses' exodus set his people free,
  Elijah's was a striking passage
    into God's better world.
Jesus' exodus wins eternal life
  through painful death upon his cross
    and glorious resurrection.

Enraptured, Peter would remain forever,
  o'ershadowed by the Lord who calls,
    "Listen to my Chosen One!"

O Father, Lord of heaven and earth,
  I will listen to your Christ—
    your own dear *saving Son!*

Lk 9:37-43 = Mk 9:14-27 Jesus heals a boy possessed by a demon.

The Least among You Is the Greatest

Lk 9:43-48: *He said to his disciples, "Let these words sink into your ears: The Son of Man is going to be betrayed into human hands." But they did not understand this saying; its meaning was concealed from them, so that they could not perceive it. And they were afraid to ask him about this saying.*

An argument arose among them as to which one of them was the greatest. But Jesus, aware of their inner thoughts, took a little child and put it by his side, and said to them, "Whoever welcomes this child in my name welcomes me, and whoever welcomes me welcomes the one who sent me; for the least among all of you is the greatest."

To contemplate:

Shortly after his transfiguration,
   he insists in strongest terms,
"The Son of Man will be betrayed!"
   But they do not understand.

Then they betray the Son of Man,
    by betraying their callousness
in their ambition to surpass,
    though he urged them bear his cross.

They try to hide from him their pride,
    but he sees into their thoughts,
the hidden corners of their minds—
    they cannot hide from him.

He tries once more to change their hearts
    with true humility,
break down the barriers they erect
    to the simple truths he tells.

At his side he puts a little child
    as example to be learned:
"Who welcomes this child in my name
    welcomes my Father and me."

O Jesus, simple as little child,
    you cut right through our pride.
I welcome you with all my heart,
    by welcoming each child!

O heavenly Father, welcome me,
    into your loving arms!

Lk 9:49-50 = Mk 9:38-40 "Whoever is not against you is for you."

Jesus Begins His Final Journey

Lk 9:51-56: *When the days drew near for him to be taken up, he set his face to go to Jerusalem. And he sent messengers ahead of him. On their way they entered a village of the Samaritans to make ready for him; but they did not receive him, because his face was set toward Jerusalem. When his disciples James and John saw it, they said, "Lord, do you want us to command fire to come down from heaven and consume them?" But he turned and rebuked them. Then they went on to another village.*

To contemplate:

As the day to meet his death draws near,
   he sets his face toward Jerusalem.
The face that shone on the glory mount
   tightens now in firm resolve.
To quicken this last trip he'd go
   directly through Samaria,
not cross to the far side of the Jordan,
   as prudent Jews would do.

First his disciples prepare the way—
    Samaritans, hostile to the Jews,
will not let Jesus through their land;
    they reject the very Lord of life!
Long years ago a Samaritan king
    sent soldiers to arrest Elijah;
the rejected prophet called down fire
    to consume the captain and his men
        (2 Kings 1:10).
Remembering this, our James and John
    ask Jesus to let them do the same
to those who now stand in his way.
    Will Jesus be a new Elijah?
No, he's a different kind of prophet,
    not one who comes with fire or sword;
a gentle Lord, restraining those
    who would destroy destroyers.

O Jesus, you never forced a heart
    to accept or honor you or yours;
give us your spirit of gentleness
    toward those who barricade our way.
As you respect our freedom, Lord,
    to choose or not to follow you,
grant us the grace to share your love
    for those who block our path.

Homeless

Lk 9:57-62: *As they were going along the road, someone said to him, "I will follow you wherever you go." And Jesus said to him, "Foxes have holes, and birds of the air have nests; but the Son of Man has nowhere to lay his head." To another he said, "Follow me." But he said, "Lord, first let me go and bury my father." But Jesus said to him, "Let the dead bury their own dead; but as for you, go and proclaim the kingdom of God." Another said, "I will follow you, Lord; but let me first say farewell to those at my home." Jesus said to him, "No one who puts a hand to the plow and looks back is fit for the kingdom of God."*

To contemplate:

Lord, you could have had more followers
   had you not been so demanding,
     so unbending.
Yet before you required another's sacrifice,
   you endured it first yourself
     in greater measure.

You asked no one to share your homelessness,
　　until you had first experienced
　　　　homelessness.
You asked no one to leave his father and mother
　　until you had first abandoned
　　　　your own sweet home.

You asked no one to put his hand to your plow
　　until you had first set out
　　　　upon your mission.

Yet it does not sound like your own voice to say,
　　"Let the dead bury their dead!
　　　　No farewells!"

Unless you are laying down priorities:
　　"Nothing precedes God's kingdom—
　　　　it must come first.
To proclaim the kingdom of God must supersede
　　even a father's burial
　　　　or fond farewell."

O homeless Lord, your values are not ours;
　　you turn us upside down,
　　　　inside out!

　　Grant us your vision, Lord!

Jesus Sends Disciples
to Proclaim the Kingdom

Lk 10:1-9: *After this the Lord appointed seventy others and sent them on ahead of him in pairs to every town and place where he himself intended to go. He said to them, "The harvest is plentiful, but the laborers are few; therefore ask the Lord of the harvest to send out laborers into his harvest. Go on your way. See, I am sending you out like lambs into the midst of wolves. Carry no purse, no bag, no sandals; and greet no one on the road. Whatever house you enter, first say, 'Peace to this house!' And if anyone is there who shares in peace, your peace will rest on that person; but if not, it will return to you. Remain in the same house, eating and drinking whatever they provide, for the laborer deserves to be paid. Do not move about from house to house. Whenever you enter a town and its people welcome you, eat what is set before you; cure the sick who are there, and say to them, 'The kingdom of God has come near to you.'"*

To contemplate:

The Lord of the harvest
   sends his workers out
     to gather it in.
   He gives them no gold,
     allows them no ease,
   sends them like lambs among wolves.
Their unique mission
   is to bring not plenty
     but peace to each house.
   Without such peace,
     his own great peace
   cannot enter in nor remain.
The kingdom of God
   is a realm of peace—
     not power but peace.
   The kingdom worker
     is a lamb, not a wolf:
   he demands nothing,
     accepts all trials.
He says few words:
   Only "peace" and "God,"
     "kingdom" and "peace."
   He preaches by acts of simple life.
   Dear Lord, let me
     your worker be.

Lk 10:10-15 = Mt 10:14-15; 11:20-24 Jesus warns those who reject his messengers.

Jesus' Joy in His Disciples' Work

Lk 10:16-20: *"Whoever listens to you listens to me, and whoever rejects you rejects me, and whoever rejects me rejects the one who sent me."*

The seventy returned with joy, saying, "Lord, in your name even the demons submit to us!" He said to them, "I watched Satan fall from heaven like a flash of lightning. See, I have given you authority to tread on snakes and scorpions, and over all the power of the enemy; and nothing will hurt you. Nevertheless, do not rejoice at this, that the spirits submit to you, but rejoice that your names are written in heaven."

To contemplate:

"Whoever listens to you,
      listens to me."
   But only if we say your words!
"Whoever rejects you,
      rejects also me."
   But only if we do your deeds!

The seventy said your words,
    did your deeds,
  and they returned to you rejoicing.
You watched them topple Satan
    from up on high
  by freeing people from his sway.

As you sent forth your seventy,
    send us forth, too,
  for we would your harvesters be.
Send us to free your people, Lord,
    your suffering folk,
  from the poison in our world.
And as you send us forth, O Lord,
    to tell of you,
  protect us from the venom,
the toxin of the evil Satan
    and his snakes—
  the poisoners of our world.

O Lord of the harvest,
    write my name—
  write it in heaven's book.
Dear Lord of the harvest,
    inscribe my name
  within your sacred heart!

Jesus Rejoices in the Holy Spirit

Lk 10:21-24: *At that same hour Jesus rejoiced in the Holy Spirit and said, "I thank you, Father, Lord of heaven and earth, because you have hidden these things from the wise and the intelligent and have revealed them to infants; yes, Father, for such was your gracious will. All things have been handed over to me by my Father; and no one knows who the Son is except the Father, or who the Father is except the Son and anyone to whom the Son chooses to reveal him."*

Then turning to the disciples, Jesus said to them privately, "Blessed are the eyes that see what you see! For I tell you that many prophets and kings desired to see what you see, but did not see it, and to hear what you hear, but did not hear it."

To contemplate:

Jesus rejoices in the Holy Spirit,
    source of all true joy.
His gaze pierces impenetrable sky
    to find his Father there,
        Lord of heaven and earth.

His prayer is like no other's prayer,
    addressing God as "Father."
The great Lord of heaven and earth,
    all-powerful Creator-God,
    is Jesus' loving Father!

On intimate terms of filial love,
    he thanks his Father-God,
thanks God for sending him
    to the simple and the poor,
    the humble and the child.
Only the Son knows the Father
    and Father knows the Son—
incomprehensible to the shrewd,
    beyond the grasp of sage;
    but the simple still believe.

Simple fathers and simple sons,
    simple mothers and their daughters,
can know the inner life of God:
    Father-God and Son-God
    love-unified in Spirit-God.
Simple folk know Jesus' God,
    and spring beyond all reason's bonds
in one single leap of faith
    in the word of the Word of God,
    in the spirit of the Spirit of God.
Lord, launch me into this great leap!

The Great Commandment

Lk 10:25-28: *Just then a lawyer stood up to test Jesus. "Teacher," he said, "what must I do to inherit eternal life?" He said to him, "What is written in the law? What do you read there?" He answered, "You shall love the Lord your God with all your heart, and with all your soul, and with all your strength, and with all your mind; and your neighbor as yourself." And he said to him, "You have given the right answer; do this, and you will live."*

To contemplate:

This lawyer's mind runs deep;
   the question that he asks
      concerns no trifling theme,
   aims at eternity:
      "How enter eternal life?"
Jesus, the greatest teacher,
   does not directly answer
      but prompts the questioner
   to answer his own query,
      explore the truth himself.

Now where would a lawyer look?
Within the law, of course!
Among the Torah's precepts
he finds an answer most profound:
"Only love is a lasting thing—
love of God complete enough
to include deep neighbor-love:
Love God and love your neighbor
in one all-embracing love.
True love of our true God
includes what he esteems—
men and women he has made."
This answer delights the teacher:
"You have very truly said!
Do this and you will live,
live eternally
in love with God and neighbor."

Jesus, your God, the God of Israel, is love!
But I, of little faith,
am also of tepid love.
Let your love live in me—
your love of God and neighbor!

The Good Samaritan

Lk 10:29-37: *But wanting to justify himself, he [the lawyer] asked Jesus, "And who is my neighbor?" Jesus replied, "A man was going down from Jerusalem to Jericho, and fell into the hands of robbers, who stripped him, beat him, and went away, leaving him half dead. Now by chance a priest was going down that road; and when he saw him, he passed by on the other side. So likewise a Levite, when he came to the place and saw him, passed by on the other side. But a Samaritan while traveling came near him; and when he saw him, he was moved with pity. He went to him and bandaged his wounds, having poured oil and wine on them. Then he put him on his own animal, brought him to an inn, and took care of him. The next day he took out two denarii, gave them to the innkeeper, and said, 'Take care of him; and when I come back, I will repay you whatever more you spend.' Which of these three, do you think, was a neighbor to the man who fell into the hands of the robbers?" He said, "The one who showed him mercy." Jesus said to him, "Go and do likewise."*

To contemplate:

This lawyer answered sagely
   that love is the central law;
      but he complicates his case
   with yet another question
      to display his inquiring mind:
"And just who is my neighbor?
   Any fellow Jew, of course—
      but also any Gentile?
   Does God want us to love
      even Samaritans?"

Instead of "Yes" or "No,"
   Jesus tells the crowd a story
      in which the questioner
   will find an answer true,
      if only he thinks it through:
The wounded Jerusalem man
   must certainly be a Jew.
      But priest and Levite ignore him;
   one lone Samaritan
      stops to care for him.
The flabbergasted lawyer
   cannot save his case,
      admits the Samaritan
   is the one who truly loves.
      "Now will you do the same?"

O Lord of universal love,
   help us love as you!

Mary Has Chosen the Better Part

Lk 10:38-42: *Now as they went on their way, he entered a certain village, where a woman named Martha welcomed him into her home. She had a sister named Mary, who sat at the Lord's feet and listened to what he was saying. But Martha was distracted by her many tasks; so she came to him and asked, "Lord, do you not care that my sister has left me to do all the work by myself? Tell her then to help me." But the Lord answered her, "Martha, Martha, you are worried and distracted by many things; there is need of only one thing. Mary has chosen the better part, which will not be taken away from her."*

To contemplate:

We watch two sisters serve you, Lord,
    one in action, one in prayer.
Both ways are good, but one is better—
    Jesus, tell us which.
Martha welcomes you into her home,
    but absorbed in diligent work,

complains about the idle Mary
  who only sits and listens.
"If this poor world depends on Mary,
  nothing will ever get done!
If you, Lord, depend on Mary,
  will your cause ever be won?"

Surprisingly you answer "Yes!
  Mary has chosen the better part;
it will not be taken away from her—
  prayer does more than work!"
Lord, you confound our ways again,
  upset our every bent—
we work so hard and yet you say
  it's better to sit and pray.

Saint Martha, teach us how to work,
  yet learn what you have learned
from the Lord who told you not to fret
  but work on tranquilly.
Saint Mary, teach us how to pray
  by sitting at his feet—
instead of doing so much talk,
  just listen to his word.

O Lord of action, Lord of prayer,
teach me to work wholeheartedly
  and rest my heart in you!

Jesus Teaches Us How to Pray

Lk 11:1-4: *He was praying in a certain place, and after he had finished, one of his disciples said to him, "Lord, teach us to pray, as John taught his disciples." He said to them, "When you pray, say:*
> *Father, hallowed be your name.*
> *Your kingdom come.*
> *Give us each day our daily bread.*
> *And forgive us our sins,*
> *for we ourselves forgive everyone indebted to us.*
> *And do not bring us to the time of trial."*

To contemplate:

O Jesus, do you who call God "Father,"
  bid us call him "Father," too?

Then God, your name to me is "Father"—
  what a holy name to say!
May all men and women bless your name,
  hallow your name of "Father."

O Father, you are the God of all.
    The angels call you "Lord,"
but in Jesus I may call you "Father";
    in him you call me "child"!

You are the Lord of heaven above,
    adored for your great might.
May your kingdom come upon our earth—
    your sway of love and light.

Give us each day our daily bread,
    the staple of our food;
give us, too, your nourishing word,
    and the bread of life to eat.

Father, forgive us all our sins,
    the sins that kill our love,
and those that distance us from you;
    we ask your pardon, Lord.

We prove our love by forgiving those
    who owe us a debt of love.
And we ask to be excused of trial,
    for we do not trust ourselves
    to stand firmly in your love.

Pray with Insistence

Lk 11:5-8: *And he said to them, "Suppose one of you has a friend, and you go to him at midnight and say to him, 'Friend, lend me three loaves of bread; for a friend of mine has arrived, and I have nothing to set before him.' And he answers from within, 'Do not bother me; the door has already been locked, and my children are with me in bed; I cannot get up and give you anything.' I tell you, even though he will not get up and give him anything because he is his friend, at least because of his persistence he will get up and give him whatever he needs."*

To contemplate:

Who else but Jesus dares to tell this story?
   Who so familiar with his God
      he can represent him
   as a father, tucked in for the night
      with his children in his bed?
Who else but Jesus dares to speak of God
   as impatient Father, too annoyed
      to respond to urgent prayer,
   too enveloped in his own repose
      to bother himself for us?

Who else but Jesus can tell us to insist
   the way this fellow in need of bread
      demands service of his friend,
   the only friend who can supply
      the bread for him this night?
Who else but Jesus dares depict our God
   as one who must be forced to act
      by insistent supplication
   to do a good deed for a friend
      in merely trifling need?
Not a flattering picture of our God?
   Ah, look again and see the Father
      in bed with all his children.
   See the amazing intimacy
      of Jesus with his Father!

Not a noble notion of our prayer?
   Look again and see the point:
      the value of persistence.
   If we are made in God's own image,
      he dwells in our best selves.

Jesus, truest image of our Father,
   help us glimpse him in our zeal
      to fulfill our neighbor's needs.

The Greatest Gift of All

Lk 11:9-13: *"So I say to you, ask, and it will be given you; search, and you will find; knock, and the door will be opened for you. For everyone who asks receives, and everyone who searches finds, and for everyone who knocks, the door will be opened. Is there anyone among you who, if your child asks for a fish, will give a snake instead of a fish? Or if the child asks for an egg, will give a scorpion? If you then, who are evil, know how to give good gifts to your children, how much more will the heavenly Father give the Holy Spirit to those who ask him!"*

To contemplate:

"Ask, search, knock...
   Whoever asks, receives;
   whoever searches, finds;
   whoever knocks, enters."
What promises, Lord, you make to us—
   so sure of your Father's love!
We are the children of his love;
   he will provide for us.

We could never *gain* salvation;
    but we can ask for it,
    search and knock for it—
and our Father opens it to us!
We must desire enough to ask,
    want enough to search,
    risk enough to knock—
    care enough to act.

If we, made in his image,
    give what is good to our children,
not poisonous snakes or scorpions,
    will he not give us his gifts?
He's given the gift of life;
    he longs to complete that gift.
But he waits for us to ask for it,
    search for it, knock for it.

It is the gift of greater life,
    life in himself, life with him—
eternal life in his Holy Spirit.
    He will not settle for a lesser gift.
More than we want to ask, he wants to give;
more than we search for him, he searches for us;
more eagerly than we knock, he opens to us—
    his gift of his Holy Spirit!

Lk 11:14-23 = Mk 3:20-27: "He casts out demons by Beelzebul."
Lk 11:24-26 = Mt 12:43-45 Jesus warns that an unclean spirit may
return with others.

True Blessedness

Lk 11:27-28: *While he was saying this, a woman in the crowd raised her voice and said to him, "Blessed is the womb that bore you and the breasts that nursed you!" But he said, "Blessed rather are those who hear the word of God and obey it!"*

To contemplate:

This woman heard him say the truths
   she'd never heard before—
thoughts far beyond her other thoughts,
   loves beyond all her loves.
He opened her mind to new ideas,
   her heart to greater depths.
He moved her beyond the narrow limits
   she thought her boundaries.
And she responded generously,
   as heartily as she could,
by praising the one who gave him life—
   his nourishing, blessed mother.

Instinctively she knew a truth:
  he was a perfect son
who would be more greatly pleased
  by praise of his mother
    than of himself.

In response he now transports her thought
  from body into spirit.
Her faith made Mary greatly blessed,
  more than her bodily service;
he praises Mary's obedient spirit
  in service of her God.
For she had listened more than the rest
  to the inner word of God;
more than all others she had heard
  and lovingly responded.
She, more than all the other maids,
  had listened to God's word,
cherished it in her loving heart
  as his special word to her.

Sweet Mary, my Lord's tender mother,
  I, too, would give him praise—
    by praising you!

Lk 11:29-32 = Mt 12:38-42 "A greater than Solomon is here."
Lk 11:33-36 = Mt 6:22-23 "Light up the way for others."
Lk 11:37-54 = Mt 23:1-36 Jesus denounces Pharisees and lawyers.
Lk 12:1-12 = Mt 10:26-33 "Have courage in time of persecution."

Jesus Rejects Greed

Lk 12:13-21: *Someone in the crowd said to him, "Teacher, tell my brother to divide the family inheritance with me." But he said to him, "Friend, who set me to be a judge or arbitrator over you?" And he said to them, "Take care! Be on your guard against all kinds of greed; for one's life does not consist in the abundance of possessions." Then he told them a parable: "The land of a rich man produced abundantly. And he thought to himself, 'What should I do, for I have no place to store my crops?' Then he said, 'I will do this: I will pull down my barns and build larger ones, and there I will store all my grain and my goods. And I will say to my soul, 'Soul, you have ample goods laid up for many years; relax, eat, drink, be merry.' But God said to him, 'You fool! This very night your life is being demanded of you. And the things you have prepared, whose will they be?' So it is with those who store up treasures for themselves but are not rich toward God."*

To contemplate:

What is this life we live—
   a time to gather goods,

a chance to expand our wealth,
leisure to enjoy our things?
"Much more than all of these!"
exclaims the author of life.
Jesus comes not to resolve
our petty litigations.
No arbiter of family quarrels,
he lifts us above our greed,
transposes a lowly question
into a higher realm.
What would he say to us today
of immersion in our things,
our stress and strain for body-bliss
to neglect of soul-content?
His parable says it all for us:
"Don't waste your precious life
on trifles of but passing worth;
raise your perspective high,
high enough to reach the sky,
not grovel on the earth;
high enough to reach our God—
everlasting life with him."
Jesus, my Lord, instill in me
your eternal view of life!

Lk 12:22-32 = Mt 6:25-34 *"Do not worry; trust in your heavenly Father."*
Lk 12:35-46 = Mt 24:43-51 *"Be his vigilant and faithful servants."*

Jesus Longs to Complete His Mission

Lk 12:49-53: *"I came to bring fire to the earth, and how I wish it were already kindled! I have a baptism with which to be baptized, and what stress I am under until it is completed! Do you think that I have come to bring peace to the earth? No, I tell you, but rather division! From now on five in one household will be divided, three against two and two against three; they will be divided:*
> *father against son and son against father,*
>> *mother against daughter and daughter against mother,*
> *mother-in-law against her daughter-in-law and daughter-in-law against mother-in-law."*

To contemplate:

O Jesus, you are no tame reformer,
   but a fiery revolutionary!
You came to a tired and dried out earth,
   came to fire it into action.
Our earth is still a tired old place
   of compromising tolerance.

What care we for absolutes
   permitting no negotiation?
Why not ignore grave aberration
   rather than struggle for truth?
Easier to invent new fraudulent names
   for harsh realities!

But you, O Lord, can hardly await
   your baptism of blood on Calvary,
to awaken our world to absolutes
   worth suffering and dying for.
Your cross will become a sign for all,
   a sign to be embraced by some,
rejected by others—as Simeon said,
   you are history's pivot-point:
families split apart over you—
   not because you split them up,
but because some members welcome you,
   while others love you not.
Thus, you who came to bring us peace
   have become a sign of division.
between those who love and those who hate.

   May I stand with those who love!

Lk 12:54-56 = Mt 16:2-3 "Interpret the signs of the times."
Lk 12:57-59 = Mt 5:25-26 "Settle with your opponent before the judgment."

God Does Not Cause Our Suffering

Luke 13:1-5: *At that very time there were some present who told him about the Galileans whose blood Pilate had mingled with their sacrifices. He asked them, "Do you think that because these Galileans suffered in this way they were worse sinners than all other Galileans? No, I tell you; but unless you repent, you will all perish as they did. Or those eighteen who were killed when the tower of Siloam fell on them—do you think that they were worse offenders than all the others living in Jerusalem? No, I tell you; but unless you repent, you will all perish just as they did."*

To contemplate:

"God smiles on us with rain,
   frowns on us with drought,
rewards our doing good with wealth,
   punishes evil with poverty;
whatever happens is God's work"—
   many might say,
applying God's work of providence
   to everything that occurs.

When Pilate killed these Jews
   in their act of sacrifice,
some held God responsible
   for punishing secret sins.

But you, my Lord, know that God
   loves too much to kill.
You give us a true picture,
   guide us to see aright:
"Don't blame God for Pilate's rage,
   abuse of his own free will.
And don't blame God for accidents
   due to your shoddy work.
God's providence gives life, not death;
   he wills our good, not harm.
If death is the cost of original sin
   in which we have a share,
then God is not the cause of death;
   sin is that cause—sin!"
O Jesus, I want to repent my sins,
   not just to escape
eternal death
   but out of love for you.

For my sins against you and others,
   forgive me, Lord.

Jesus Cares for Us

Lk 13:6-9: *Then he told this parable: "A man had a fig tree planted in his vineyard; and he came looking for fruit on it and found none. So he said to the gardener, 'See here! For three years I have come looking for fruit on this fig tree, and still I find none. Cut it down! Why should it be wasting the soil?' He replied, 'Sir, let it alone for one more year, until I dig around it and put manure on it. If it bears fruit next year, well and good; but if not, you can cut it down.'"*

To contemplate:

For three short years has Jesus worked
   in the orchard of his Father.
For three long years has the Father watched,
   awaiting good results.
But what about this barren tree,
   bearing no fruit of love.
Leaves, appearance of life, it bears,
   but not a fig to eat.

What farmer would abide such tree,
   allow it to take up ground
good for some other tree or crop—
   what good to let it be?
And so the Father commands his Son
   to cut down the worthless tree;
but the Son implores his Father-God
   to let him try once more.

An image of our saving Lord
   who never abandons us,
the gardener who graces us,
   even when we fail.
In compassion he stoops down to us,
   bears our cold indifference,
pleads for us to our heavenly Father,
   and works once more with us.

And we—do we respond to him
   with continued apathy?
O Jesus, great horticulturist,
   stir up my dying roots.
Fill my mind with your holy thoughts,
   my heart with your holy love;
permeate my very soul
   with the love of your sacred heart!

Jesus Cures a Woman
on the Sabbath

Lk 13:10-17: *Now he was teaching in one of the synagogues on the sabbath. And just then there appeared a woman with a spirit that had crippled her for eighteen years. She was bent over and was quite unable to stand up straight. When Jesus saw her, he called her over and said, "Woman, you are set free from your ailment." When he laid his hands on her, immediately she stood up straight and began praising God. But the leader of the synagogue, indignant because Jesus had cured on the sabbath, kept saying to the crowd, "There are six days on which work ought to be done; come on those days and be cured, and not on the sabbath day." But the Lord answered him and said, "You hypocrites! Does not each of you on the sabbath untie his ox or his donkey from the manger, and lead it away to give it water? And ought not this woman, a daughter of Abraham whom Satan bound for eighteen long years, be set free from this bondage on the sabbath day?" When he said this, all his opponents were put to shame; and the entire crowd was rejoicing at all the wonderful things that he was doing.*

To contemplate:

The Image of the Father's love,
    lifts up a bent old woman,
        frees her of crippling pain.
Thus Jesus shows the providence
    by which God lifts us up
        from bondage to our sins.

The leaders do not see the cure,
    only that he broke the law.

But his great compassion is not lost
    upon the curious crowd:
        they rejoice at his good deed.

O Jesus, we thank you for your cure
    of this daughter of Abraham,
        suffering from Satan's curse.

We confess to you our own distress,
    in hope you'll stoop to us
        with compassionate intent.

Lord of the afflicted, Lord of pain,
    have mercy on us all—
        heal us with your love.

Lk 13:18-21 = Mt 13:31-33 The parables of the mustard seed and of the yeast.
Lk 13:22-30 = Mt 7:13-14, 21-23; 8:11-12; 19:20 "Enter through the narrow door."

Jesus Holds to His Mission Out of Love

Lk 13:31-35: *Some Pharisees came and said to him, "Get away from here, for Herod wants to kill you." He said to them, "Go and tell that fox for me, 'Listen, I am casting out demons and performing cures today and tomorrow, and on the third day I finish my work. Yet today, tomorrow, and the next day I must be on my way, because it is impossible for a prophet to be killed outside of Jerusalem.' Jerusalem, Jerusalem, the city that kills the prophets and stones those who are sent to it! How often have I desired to gather your children together as a hen gathers her brood under her wings, and you were not willing! See, your house is left to you. And I tell you, you will not see me until the time comes when you say, 'Blessed is the one who comes in the name of the Lord.'"*

To contemplate:

Today, tomorrow, and on the next of days—
    every day you'll be the same, my Lord.
Every day you'll cast out evil demons,
    perform your cures, especially for the poor;

and you will promptly end your work and die.
   Your death will end your work of saving us
in Jerusalem, the place where prophets die—
   much more than prophet, you, O saving Lord!

O Jesus, take us under your outstretched arm
   to receive the inflow of your gracious care.
You grieved for Jerusalem,
   its house to be left desolate.
Yet Lord, Jerusalem will welcome you:
   "Blessed be he who comes in the name of the
      Lord!"
But within the lapse of a few fast fleeting days,
   they'll shout, "Crucify him! Crucify him!"
You know that, Lord, and yet you press right on,
   on to Jerusalem, though there you'll die
to complete your monumental enterprise
   to save the world from monumental sin.

Today, tomorrow, and on the next of days—
   every day of my life, my dearest Lord,
may I press on toward your new Jerusalem
   of life with you and your loving Father-God!

Jesus Cures a Man on the Sabbath

Lk 14:1-6: *On one occasion when Jesus was going to the house of a leader of the Pharisees to eat a meal on the sabbath, they were watching him closely. Just then, in front of him, there was a man who had dropsy. And Jesus asked the lawyers and Pharisees, "Is it lawful to cure people on the sabbath, or not?" But they were silent. So Jesus took him and healed him, and sent him away. Then he said to them, "If one of you has a child or an ox that has fallen into a well, will you not immediately pull it out on a sabbath day?" And they could not reply to this.*

To contemplate:

They watched you closely, Lord,
   yet nothing did they see
      of what you really did.
They sat in solemn judgment
   over you, their greatest judge,
      watching your every move.

You cured a man of dropsy,
   but these men only saw
      you break the sabbath law.

How could they not see?
How could they fail to grasp
the truth of what you did?

Yet here am I, still blind
to the deepest inner truth
of what you do for me.
I seem to live on the rim
of a life much too profound
for me to comprehend.
I touch only the skin,
fail to enter the core
of life that reaches God.

But you, dear Lord, penetrate
straight to the very point—
the meaning of each new moment.
Your compassion cuts clean through
circumstantial fluff,
to embrace at once the heart.

O Lord of all our suffering,
open my eyes at last!
Give me compassion, Lord!

Jesus Challenges Our Generosity

Lk 14:7-14: *When he noticed how the guests chose the places of honor, he told them a parable. "When you are invited by someone to a wedding banquet, do not sit down at the place of honor, in case someone more distinguished than you has been invited by your host; and the host who invited both of you may come and say to you, 'Give this person your place,' and then in disgrace you would start to take the lowest place. But when you are invited, go and sit down at the lowest place, so that when your host comes, he may say to you, 'Friend, move up higher'; then you will be honored in the presence of all who sit at the table with you. For all who exalt themselves will be humbled, and those who humble themselves will be exalted."*

He said also to the one who had invited him, "When you give a luncheon or a dinner, do not invite your friends or your brothers or your relatives or rich neighbors, in case they may invite you in return, and you would be repaid. But when you give a banquet, invite the poor, the crippled, the lame, and the blind. And you will be blessed, because they cannot repay you, for you will be repaid at the resurrection of the righteous."

To contemplate:

Dear Lord, you will not compromise
    with their most natural bent.
Their nature seeks a higher place,
    but you tell them to take a lower one,
    the lowest place of all!
Ah, you are really clever, Lord;
    you advise the lowest place
that they may be moved higher up,
    exalted in the eyes of all
    of those who watch them rise.

Clever or just realistic, Lord?
    Your appeal is to these lawyers
who cannot understand incentive
    higher than the one you offer—
    they want acknowledgment.
For when you speak of inviting the poor,
    who can't reciprocate,
you clarify the act you praise:
    not spurious ingenuity,
    but true humility.

Dear Lord, if I follow every whim,
    how can I deny myself
the higher place that holds me up
    to admiring gaze of all?

Lord, save me from myself!

The Great Feast of Heaven

Lk 14:15-24: *One of the dinner guests...said to him, "Blessed is anyone who will eat bread in the kingdom of God!" Then Jesus said to him, "Someone gave a great dinner and invited many. At the time for the dinner he sent his slave to say to those who had been invited, 'Come; for everything is ready now.' But they all alike began to make excuses. The first said to him, 'I have bought a piece of land, and I must go out and see it; please accept my regrets.' Another said, 'I have bought five yoke of oxen, and I am going to try them out; please accept my regrets.' Another said, 'I have just been married, and therefore I cannot come.' So the slave returned and reported this to his master. Then the owner of the house became angry and said to his slave, 'Go out at once into the streets and lanes of the town and bring in the poor, the crippled, the blind, and the lame.' And the slave said, 'Sir, what you ordered has been done, and there is still room.' Then the master said to the slave, 'Go out into the roads and lanes, and compel people to come in, so that my house may be filled. For I tell you, none of those who were invited will taste my dinner.'"*

To contemplate:

Your challenge in our day is still the same.
   Have not we always been immersed
     in temporal affairs,
     for which we excuse ourselves
   from giving time to God?
Now our gadgets absorb our precious time,
   or shopping in department stores,
     or driving north or south,
     or running east or west,
   or lounging home before TV.

Our work's too urgent to give us time for prayer;
   our play and pleasure too engaging,
     our leisure too confined,
     our trifles too important
   to allow us time for your banquet, Lord.
It's the age-old story of our priorities;
   we've got them badly twisted,
     confusing first with second,
     replacing last with first,
   and substituting wrong for right.

Dear Lord, will our places, too, be given to others?
   What tragedy to miss the goal of life,
     exchange the great for small,
     the lasting for the passing,
   forget the purpose of all our living!
   Lord, move us with your grace!

Jesus Challenges Our Love

Lk 14:25-35: *Now large crowds were traveling with him; and he turned and said to them, "Whoever comes to me and does not hate father and mother, wife and children, brothers and sisters, yes, and even life itself, cannot be my disciple. Whoever does not carry the cross and follow me cannot be my disciple. For which of you, intending to build a tower, does not first sit down and estimate the cost, to see whether he has enough to complete it? Otherwise, when he...is not able to finish, all who see it will begin to ridicule him, saying, 'This fellow began to build and was not able to finish.' Or what king, going out to wage war against another king, will not sit down first and consider whether he is able with ten thousand to oppose the one who comes against him with twenty thousand? If he cannot, then, while the other is still far away, he sends a delegation and asks for the terms of peace. So therefore, none of you can become my disciple if you do not give up all your possessions."*

"Salt is good; but if salt has lost its taste, how can its saltiness be restored? It is fit neither for the soil nor for the manure pile; they throw it away. Let anyone with ears to hear listen!"

To contemplate:

"Hate your father and mother, wife and children."
  Lord, did you really say these words?
    Not without a context:
  "Whoever does not carry the cross
and follow me, cannot be my disciple."
Is it possible to see our relationships,
  all our plans and all our actions,
    in terms of following you?
  How can we give up all possessions
and still have life and vigor to follow you?

Or do you here express vague figures of speech
  bereft of more than relative meaning?
    How can we be indifferent
  to father, mother, wife and child,
and ready to give up all that we possess?
I think you really would have us be detached
  from all the things that we possess,
    but very much concerned
  about the persons in our lives—
you commanded us to love them as ourselves.

O Jesus, help me love you so completely
  in mother, father, wife and child,
    that my love for them
  spreads out to all the world,
gives meaning to my work to build your tower.

Parables Urging Repentance

Lk 15:1-10: *Now all the tax collectors and sinners were coming near to listen to him. And the Pharisees and the scribes were grumbling and saying, "This fellow welcomes sinners and eats with them."*

So he told them this parable: "Which one of you, having a hundred sheep and losing one of them, does not leave the ninety-nine in the wilderness and go after the one that is lost until he finds it? When he has found it, he lays it on his shoulders and rejoices. And when he comes home, he calls together his friends and neighbors, saying to them, 'Rejoice with me, for I have found my sheep that was lost.' Just so, I tell you, there will be more joy in heaven over one sinner who repents than over ninety-nine righteous persons who need no repentance.

"Or what woman having ten silver coins, if she loses one of them, does not light a lamp, sweep the house, and search carefully until she finds it? When she has found it, she calls together her friends and neighbors, saying, 'Rejoice with me, for I have found the coin that I had lost.' Just so, I tell you, there is joy in the presence of the angels of God over one sinner who repents."

To contemplate:

Lord of parables,
out of the actions of our lives
you weave a pattern of eternal meaning:

A sheep is lost;
you build the event into the drama
of a person struggling between heaven and hell.

A coin is lost;
you work the occurrence into a story
of the joy of angels over a sinner's repentance.

Thus you teach us
the inner meaning of our lives,
their sovereign value in the sight of God.

And thus you welcome
lost sinners and even eat with them.
What could a Savior do were there none to save?

Lord, here is one—
a lost sheep, lost coin, lost sinner,
who desperately needs your saving ministry.

Compassionate Lord,
stretch out to me your saving hand,
hold me close to your heart of saving love!

The Prodigal Son

Lk 15:11-24: *Then Jesus said, "There was a man who had two sons. The younger of them said,... 'Father, give me the share of the property that will belong to me.' So he divided his property between them. A few days later the younger son...traveled to a distant country, and there he squandered his property in dissolute living. When he had spent everything, a severe famine took place.... So he went and hired himself out to one of the citizens of that country, who sent him to his fields to feed the pigs. He would gladly have filled himself with the pods that the pigs were eating; and no one gave him anything. But when he came to himself he said, 'How many of my father's hired hands have bread enough to spare, but here I am dying of hunger! I will get up and go to my father, and I will say to him, "Father, I have sinned against heaven and before you; I am no longer worthy to be called your son; treat me like one of your hired hands."' So he set off and went to his father. But while he was still far off, his father saw him and was filled with compassion; he ran and put his arms around him and kissed him. Then the son said to him, 'Father, I have sinned against heaven and before you; I am no longer worthy to be called your son.' But the father said*

*to his slaves, 'Quickly, bring out a robe—the best one—
and put it on him; put a ring on his finger and sandals
on his feet. And get the fatted calf and kill it, and let us
eat and celebrate; for this son of mine was dead and is
alive again; he was lost and is found!' And they began to
celebrate."*

To contemplate:

This father represents our God?
    A father who dotes upon his son
enough to give him all he asks,
    even his share of inheritance.
A father who lets his son go forth
    to waste his heritage abroad.
A father who welcomes back that son
    without a question, just pure joy,
and then heaps gift after gift on him
    in prodigal celebration,
as though he deserved a great reward
    for such a profligate life!

How undignified is Jesus' God—
    utterly lacking family pride.
A lavish spoiler of his son—
    undisciplining, undisciplined!

Not the God I would conjure up
    in my wildest imagination.
O Father, how wonderful you are,
    how prodigal with us!

The Prodigal Father

Lk 15:25-32: *"Now his elder son was in the field; and when he came and approached the house, he heard music and dancing. He called one of the slaves and asked what was going on. He replied, 'Your brother has come, and your father has killed the fatted calf, because he has got him back safe and sound.' Then he became angry and refused to go in. His father came out and began to plead with him. But he answered his father, 'Listen! For all these years I have been working like a slave for you, and I have never disobeyed your command; yet you have never given me even a young goat so that I might celebrate with my friends. But when this son of yours came back, who has devoured your property with prostitutes, you killed the fatted calf for him!' Then the father said to him, 'Son, you are always with me, and all that is mine is yours. But we had to celebrate and rejoice, because this brother of yours was dead and has come to life; he was lost and has been found.'"*

To contemplate:

Neither son is worth his father's love:
    the younger fails as a prodigal;
        the elder, as a miser,
outraged at his father's lavishness—
    a miser hoarding up his hurt,
        a miser with his love.

The father is prodigal toward both his sons,
    lavish in pardon of the younger
        and endurance of the elder.

This prodigal father forgives his prodigal son,
    holds his patience with his miser son,
        and even pleads with him.

Jesus, this Father of yours is incredible!
    Can our God be so extravagant
        in conferring his forgiveness?

Lord, I believe the unbelievable:
    I believe our God is prodigal
        with his everlasting love!

Dear Father, God of Jesus' revelation,
    I am prodigal with my sins,
        miserly with my love.

I come to you as the prodigal son for pardon,
    and as the miserly son to bathe
        in your luxuriant love!

Be Shrewd in Your Master's Service

Lk 16:1-9: *Then Jesus said to the disciples, "There was a rich man who had a manager, and charges were brought to him that this man was squandering his property. So he summoned him and said to him, 'What is this that I hear about you?...you cannot be my manager any longer.' Then the manager said to himself, 'What will I do, now that my master is taking the position away from me? I am not strong enough to dig, and I am ashamed to beg. I have decided what to do so that, when I am dismissed as manager, people may welcome me into their homes.' So, summoning his master's debtors one by one, he asked the first, 'How much do you owe my master?' He answered, 'A hundred jugs of olive oil.' He said to him, 'Take your bill, sit down quickly, and make it fifty.' Then he asked another, 'And how much do you owe?' He replied, 'A hundred containers of wheat.' He said to him, 'Take your bill and make it eighty.' And his master commended the dishonest manager because he had acted shrewdly; for the children of this age are more shrewd in dealing with their own generation than are the children of light. And I tell you, make friends for yourselves by means of dishonest wealth so that when it is gone, they may welcome you into the eternal homes."*

To contemplate:

Lord Jesus, what are you telling us here?
 Do you really mean to present
 this less than honest steward
 as a model for our behavior?
Or are you indulging in irony?
The only way I can understand—
 fit these with your other words—
 is to think of your praise
 of this fraudulent steward
as aimed to shame our sluggishness.

This manager manipulates all the debtors
 as a lesson for us all
 in careful calculation
 to snatch the best result
from an otherwise great loss.
Lord, we are inefficient servants;
 we do less with eternal wealth
 than does this ingenious steward
 with the goods of this passing world
to win approbation for his diligence.

Lord Jesus, grace us with your wisdom
 to serve you with sharper mind;
 and with much more generous heart,
make each invested word bear fruit.

You Can Serve Only One Master

Lk 16:10-17: *"Whoever is faithful in a very little is faithful also in much; and whoever is dishonest in a very little is dishonest also in much. If then you have not been faithful with the dishonest wealth, who will entrust to you the true riches? And if you have not been faithful with what belongs to another, who will give you what is your own? No slave can serve two masters; for a slave will either hate the one and love the other, or be devoted to the one and despise the other. You cannot serve God and wealth."*

The Pharisees, who were lovers of money, heard all this, and they ridiculed him. So he said to them, "You are those who justify yourselves in the sight of others; but God knows your hearts; for what is prized by human beings is an abomination in the sight of God.

"The law and the prophets were in effect until John came; since then the good news of the kingdom of God is proclaimed, and everyone tries to enter it by force. But it is easier for heaven and earth to pass away, than for one stroke of a letter in the law to be dropped."

To contemplate:

God is a master; wealth is, too.
  "Choose between them," you demand.
Lord, we'd like to have it both ways—
  why can't we serve them both?

"What human beings prize, God scorns."
  How can you say such a thing?
Isn't wealth promised
  to those who obey? (Deut 28:11).
Do you now set a standard
  requiring a change of heart?

You say, "you cannot serve two masters;
  you cannot serve God and wealth."
Moses urged his people
  to set their hearts wholly on God (Deut 30:15-20).
You, Lord, also ask us to serve him
  with undivided hearts.

What is my heart set on?
Do I covet elusive wealth?
Or does God hold first place in my heart?

Lord Jesus, give me the wisdom
  to discern true riches
And the love to put you first in my heart.

Lk 16:18 = Mk 10:11-12 "Whoever divorces his wife and marries another commits adultery."

Lazarus and the Rich Man

Lk 16:19-31: *"There was a rich man who was dressed in purple and fine linen and who feasted sumptuously every day. And at his gate lay a poor man named Lazarus, covered with sores, who longed to satisfy his hunger with what fell from the rich man's table; even the dogs would come and lick his sores. The poor man died and was carried away by the angels to be with Abraham. The rich man also died and was buried. In Hades,...he looked up and saw Abraham far away with Lazarus by his side. He called out, 'Father Abraham, have mercy on me, and send Lazarus to dip the tip of his finger in water and cool my tongue; for I am in agony in these flames.' But Abraham said, 'Child, remember that during your lifetime you received your good things, and Lazarus in like manner evil things;...' He said, 'Then, father, I beg you to send him to my father's house—for I have five brothers—that he may warn them, so that they will not also come into this place of torment.' Abraham replied, 'They have Moses and the prophets; they should listen to them.' He said, 'No, father Abraham; but if someone goes to them from the dead, they will repent.' He said to him, 'If they do not listen to Moses and the prophets, neither will they be convinced even if someone rises from the dead.'"*

To contemplate:

What contrasts you paint for us in this narrative!
    First the rich man garbed in fine linen,
        the poor man clothed with sores,
        the luxurious feasting of the first,
    the craving of the second for mere scraps.
At last, both suffer the lot of all humans in death.
And here your story takes on a deeper significance.
    The previous contrast is now reversed:
        he who was rich is now poor;
        he who was poor is now rich.
    The man who ignored his neighbor suffers;
and the former sufferer rejoices with Abraham.

You draw the moral sharp as thrust of sword:
    those who disobey great Moses' law
        will utterly ignore
        your own resurrection!
    O Lord, how could you go on to die
for all of us, knowing how indifferent we are!

My Lord, am I the poor man or the rich?
    Do I ignore my suffering neighbor,
        or bear my cross with you?

Lk 17:1-2 = Mt 18:6-7 *One who gives scandal deserves a millstone around his neck.*

Lord, Increase Our Faith!

Lk 17:3-6: *"Be on your guard! If another disciple sins, you must rebuke the offender, and if there is repentance, you must forgive. And if the same person sins against you seven times a day, and turns back to you seven times and says, 'I repent,' you must forgive."*

The apostles said to the Lord, "Increase our faith!" The Lord replied, "If you had faith the size of a mustard seed, you could say to this mulberry tree, 'Be uprooted and planted in the sea,' and it would obey you."

To contemplate:

"Lord, we ask you to increase our faith!"
    To forgive, we need great faith;
to forgive another seven times a day
    we need seven times great faith.

Can someone offend me seven times a day
    and say, "I'm truly sorry"?
Do you expect me to forgive him every time
    he tramples upon my pride?

When I see how often I offend my God,
    seven times a day seems few.
Then how can I say I really repent
    and continue to fall again?

So your measurement is a lenient one,
    when I see it in this light;
no wonder I need such a merciful God
    to forgive me so many times!

Hence, I pray my Lord, "Increase my hope!"
    that my Father forgive my sins,
and forgive me again and yet again,
    and still keep on forgiving.

And I pray dear Lord, "Increase my love."
    For without far greater love,
I cannot forgive a friend seven times
    and find God's forgiveness for me.

Jesus, my most compassionate Lord,
    of faith and hope and love,
Increase my faith, my hope, my love—
    send me your forgiving Spirit!

We Are Servants Only If We Serve

Lk 17:7-10: *"Who among you would say to your slave who has just come in from plowing or tending sheep in the field, 'Come here at once and take your place at the table'? Would you not rather say to him, 'Prepare supper for me, put on your apron and serve me while I eat and drink; later you may eat and drink'? Do you thank the slave for doing what was commanded? So you also, when you have done all that you were ordered to do, say, 'We are worthless slaves; we have done only what we ought to have done!'"*

To contemplate:

Another picture drawn from life,
   but not the life we know,
      not Western life today.
Surprising image of servility,
   it makes its point by overkill:
      "We are but worthless slaves."
Is that a point we need to learn?
   We have no slavery now;
      today we value freedom!

What can we learn from anachronism?
  We abolished slavery long ago,
    yet are we all equal now?
Truly we are in such danger
  of arrogance as were those
    to whom you spoke this word.
Have we forgotten our low estate?
  Have we laid aside all reverence
    and even dignity?
Have we substituted mediocrity
  in place of true nobility
    toward one another?
Have we demoted God to democratic rank
  and treated him like any
    minor dignitary?
Have we placed ourselves instead of him
  as arbiters of right and wrong,
    with power to kill a fetus,
    or end our own lives
    when we will?

Lord Jesus, mighty Savior of our world,
  restore to us integrity—
    deep reverence for God
    as Master of our world,
    and of ourselves!

The Grateful Leper

Lk 17:11-19: *On the way to Jerusalem Jesus was going through the region between Samaria and Galilee. As he entered a village, ten lepers approached him. Keeping their distance, they called out, saying, "Jesus, Master, have mercy on us!" When he saw them, he said to them, "Go and show yourselves to the priests." And as they went, they were made clean. Then one of them, when he saw that he was healed, turned back, praising God with a loud voice. He prostrated himself at Jesus' feet and thanked him. And he was a Samaritan. Then Jesus asked, "Were not ten made clean? But the other nine, where are they? Was none of them found to return and give praise to God except this foreigner?" Then he said to him, "Get up and go on your way; your faith has made you well."*

To contemplate:

One out of ten men thanked you, Lord,
   for the miracle you worked for him.
Would our percentage now be higher?
   Are we more thankful than were they?

And he who thanked you was a Samaritan.
    "Where are the other nine?" you ask.
"Why have they not returned with you?
    Did I not cure them, too?"

You recently told a parable
    of a Good Samaritan,
the only one who helped a Jew
    waylaid by bandits bold.
And now again a foreigner
    shows greater grace.
For his attitude of gratitude
    you compliment his faith.

Of all the ten there is only one
    who receives your lordly praise—
the only one who thanked you, Lord,
    for the cure of leprosy.
Faith is foundation for the cure,
    faith motivates his thanks;
faith prostrates him before his Lord;
    and faith will save him now!

Jesus, Master, have mercy on us!
    Save us from leprosy,
the black leprosy of sinfulness.
    Save us from thanklessness—
    grant us deep faith in you!

The Kingdom of God Is among You

Lk 17:20-30: *Once Jesus was asked by the Pharisees when the kingdom of God was coming, and he answered, "The kingdom of God is not coming with things that can be observed; nor will they say, 'Look, here it is!' or 'There it is!' For, in fact, the kingdom of God is among you."*

Then he said to the disciples, "The days are coming when you will long to see one of the days of the Son of Man, and you will not see it. They will say to you, 'Look there!' or 'Look here!' Do not go, do not set off in pursuit. For as the lightning flashes and lights up the sky from one side to the other, so will the Son of Man be in his day. But first he must endure much suffering and be rejected by this generation. Just as it was in the days of Noah, so too it will be in the days of the Son of Man. They were eating and drinking, and marrying and being given in marriage, until the day Noah entered the ark, and the flood came and destroyed all of them. Likewise, just as it was in the days of Lot: they were eating and drinking, buying and selling, planting and building, but on the day that Lot left Sodom, it rained fire and sulfur from heaven and destroyed all of them—it will be like that on the day that the Son of Man is revealed."

To contemplate:

We look about our world and see
  widespread violence, sex and crime,
crass glorification of the flesh.
  Oh, where is your kingdom, Lord?
    In whose hearts do you reign?

We cannot see your kingdom, Lord,
  only the kingdom of Satan's rule;
yet you say God's kingdom is among us!
  How can you make that statement, Lord,
    in the face of the facts we see?

Our advertisers tell us where
  to look for the kingdom of happiness:
"Look there; look here"—they show us joy
  that leads to sad satiety
    with the things that pass away.

Yet we have it on your solemn word:
  God's kingdom is among us, in us—
if we only search down deep within
  and find our hearts once more.

O Son of Man, must we suffer first,
  carry the cross with you?
  O Son of Man, you lead the way
    out of our Sodom pit!

Lk 17:31-37 = Mt 24:40-41; 28 The reckoning on the last day.

The Unjust Judge and
the Insistent Widow

Lk 18:1-8: *Then Jesus told them a parable about their need to pray always and not to lose heart. He said, "In a certain city there was a judge who neither feared God nor had respect for people. In that city there was a widow who kept coming to him and saying, 'Grant me justice against my opponent.' For a while he refused; but later he said to himself, 'Though I have no fear of God and no respect for anyone, yet because this widow keeps bothering me, I will grant her justice, so that she may not wear me out by continually coming.'" And the Lord said, "Listen to what the unjust judge says. And will not God grant justice to his chosen ones who cry to him day and night? Will he delay long in helping them? I tell you, he will quickly grant justice to them. And yet, when the Son of Man comes, will he find faith on earth?"*

To contemplate:

How often would you have us pray, dear Lord?
  Two or three times a day—
    or four or five?

No, you talk about our need "to pray always
    and never to lose heart."
        Pray always!

Then you illustrate your point with a parable
    of a wicked judge conquered
        by persistence.

And you draw the moral of your little play:
    If an unjust judge listens
        to a just widow,
will not our just and loving Father-God
    hear our constant prayer
        of faith?

For faith and love prevail upon our God;
    and love justifies us
        in his eyes.

Our faith is under constant stress and strain
    in our world of little faith
        and little prayer.
If, then, we would preserve our faith always,
    we must have minds and hearts
        that pray always.

O Son of Man, Lord of faith and hope and love,
    pray deep within my heart—always!

The Pharisee and the Tax Collector

Lk 18:9-14: *He also told this parable to some who trusted in themselves that they were righteous and regarded others with contempt: "Two men went up to the temple to pray, one a Pharisee and the other a tax collector. The Pharisee, standing by himself, was praying thus, 'God, I thank you that I am not like other people: thieves, rogues, adulterers, or even like this tax collector. I fast twice a week; I give a tenth of all my income.' But the tax collector, standing far off, would not even look up to heaven, but was beating his breast and saying, 'God, be merciful to me, a sinner!' I tell you, this man went down to his home justified rather than the other; for all who exalt themselves will be humbled, but all who humble themselves will be exalted."*

To contemplate:

Which of these two men am I,
   the humble or the proud?
Do I truthfully recognize my sins,
   or self-proclaim good deeds?
Do I hide away my inmost faults
   behind the flaws of those

I find inferior to myself
  by false comparison?

O Jesus, you bare my secret self
  even unto me;
you uncover my utter hollowness
  as I stand before my God.

I put the best face on my acts,
  the worst on those of others;
thus I live self-satisfied,
  secure in my place with God,
oblivious of many thoughts and deeds
  unworthy of a follower
of the great God who humbled himself
  to become human like me (Phil 2:7-8).

Jesus, teacher of humility,
  teach me to beat my breast,
acknowledging my many sins:
  "Be merciful, God, to me!"

Ironically, we poor women and men
  aspire to replace our God;
while he, almighty God himself,
  aspired to be one of us!

_____

Lk 18:15-43 = Mk 10:13-52 Jesus blesses children, invites the rich man to follow him, and heals a blind beggar.

Jesus Converts Zacchaeus

Lk 19:1-10: *He entered Jericho and was passing through it. A man was there named Zacchaeus; he was a chief tax collector and was rich. He was trying to see who Jesus was, but on account of the crowd he could not, because he was short in stature. So he ran ahead and climbed a sycamore tree to see him, because he was going to pass that way. When Jesus came to the place, he looked up and said to him, "Zacchaeus, hurry and come down; for I must stay at your house today." So he hurried down and was happy to welcome him. All who saw it began to grumble and said, "He has gone to be the guest of one who is a sinner." Zacchaeus stood there and said to the Lord, "Look, half of my possessions, Lord, I will give to the poor; and if I have defrauded anyone of anything, I will pay back four times as much." Then Jesus said to him, "Today salvation has come to this house, because he too is a son of Abraham. For the Son of Man came to seek out and to save the lost."*

To contemplate:

Zacchaeus—may I call you saint?—
    where did you get your zest
        to see this Son of Man?
Was it curiosity or faith
    that sent you up a tree
        for the man you called your Lord?

The people hated you and laughed,
    but you didn't care a whit;
        Jesus did not laugh.
He invited you to welcome him
    into your house to stay
        a little while with you.

He exposed himself to scandal mongers
    to be awhile with you,
        and open up your heart.
How wide, at last, he opened it!
    To the poor, half your wealth;
        to the wronged, four times the wrong!

Zacchaeus, who climbed the tree,
    where would you be now
        had you not climbed that tree?

O Jesus, stay here within my home!
    You've come to save the lost;
        come, then, and save me too!

Jesus Will Return for Judgment

Luke 19:11-27: *He went on to tell a parable, because he was near Jerusalem, and because they supposed that the kingdom of God was to appear immediately. So he said, "A nobleman went to a distant country to get royal power for himself and then return. He summoned ten of his slaves, and gave them ten pounds, and said to them, 'Do business with these until I come back.' But the citizens of his country hated him and sent a delegation after him, saying, 'We do not want this man to rule over us.' When he returned, having received royal power, he ordered these slaves, to whom he had given the money, to be summoned.... The first came forward and said, 'Lord, your pound has made ten more pounds.' He said to him, 'Well done, good slave! Because you have been trustworthy in a very small thing, take charge of ten cities....' [The last] came, saying, 'Lord, here is your pound....' He said to him.... 'Why then did you not put my money into the bank? Then when I returned, I could have collected it with interest.... Take the pound from him and give it to the one who has ten pounds.... I tell you, to all those who have, more will be given; but from those who have nothing, even what they have will be taken away. But as for these enemies of mine who did not want me to be king*

over them—bring them here and slaughter them in my presence.'"

To contemplate:

Why, Lord, such severe portrait of yourself?
 You are on the point of entering Jerusalem,
last phase of the mission your Father gave to you—
 Jerusalem, the place where you will die!
You must prepare your own for what will come:
 your disciples sense the end is drawing near;
you therefore warn them that there will be a time
 between your leaving and return to rule.

During that lapse of time we must work on,
 using for gain the gifts you've left with us—
the gifts of grace you give to inspire good works
 by which we share in your own saving work.

But even worse than sloth is the sin of hate,
 the hate by which we would reject you, Lord,
refuse to recognize your right to rule
 our minds and hearts, our loves—our very lives.

How forcefully you tell us in this story, Lord,
 that if we fail to love your gentle rule
we cannot hope to enter in with you;
 without you, heaven cannot heaven be!

Dear Lord, when you return with royal power,
 empower me to enter in with you!

Jesus Approaches Jerusalem in Glory

Lk 19:29-40: *When he had come near Bethphage and Bethany, at the place called the Mount of Olives, he sent two of the disciples, saying, "Go into the village ahead of you, and as you enter it you will find tied there a colt that has never been ridden. Untie it and bring it here. If anyone asks you, 'Why are you untying it?' just say this, 'The Lord needs it.'" So those who were sent departed and found it as he had told them.... Then they brought it to Jesus; and after throwing their cloaks on the colt, they set Jesus on it. As he rode along, people kept spreading their cloaks on the road. As he was now approaching the path down from the Mount of Olives, the whole multitude of the disciples began to praise God joyfully with a loud voice for all the deeds of power that they had seen, saying,*

> *"Blessed is the king*
> > *who comes in the name of the Lord,*
> *Peace in heaven,*
> > *and glory in the highest heaven!"*

Some of the Pharisees in the crowd said to him, "Teacher, order your disciples to stop." He answered, "I tell you, if these were silent, the stones would shout out."

To contemplate:

For one brief moment before his passion,
  Jesus hints of coming glory
by approaching Jerusalem in triumph,
  hailed as the King of the Jews!
But not as the kings of earth comes he,
  riding a noble charger;
he rides upon a donkey's colt—
  a humble Lord is he!

Yet they spread their cloaks for him to tread
  and they praise God joyfully,
for they have seen God's glorious power
  in the deeds of him who comes.
Some Pharisees are scandalized
  that he lets the crowd praise him;
but in praising him they praise the God
  in whose blessed name he comes.

This glory is only a preview glimpse
  of his great coming glory:
when he returns to Bethany
  after all is said and done,
he will ascend to highest heaven,
  the new Jerusalem!
O Jesus, I, too, raise my voice
  in praise of you, my Lord!

Jesus Weeps Over Jerusalem

Lk 19:41-44: *As he came near and saw the city, he wept over it, saying, "If you, even you, had only recognized on this day the things that make for peace! But now they are hidden from your eyes. Indeed, the days will come upon you, when your enemies will set up ramparts around you and surround you, and hem you in on every side. They will crush you to the ground, you and your children within you, and they will not leave within you one stone upon another; because you did not recognize the time of your visitation from God."*

To contemplate:

Nor does our world today discern
   the things that make for peace.
We rush about in violent stress
   to gather up more wealth.
We buy ever more lethal games
   to entertain our kids,
and wonder why they turn to hate
   instead of loving trust.
Out of our schools we've thrown our God,
   confined him to the church,

and wonder why our streets are strewn
   with acts of violence.
Is there no God up there who cares
   what happens in our homes?
Is there no God who intervenes
   to save us from ourselves?

Why are you so silent, God—
   you care not a fig for us?
Not even a special thunderbolt
   to frighten us into sense?

Ah, but here are tears for us,
   tears of our dear Lord!
He weeps over Jerusalem
   and all our cities bleak.

O Jesus, thank you for these tears,
   revealing God to us,
tears that tell us more than words
   our Father's love for us.
Jerusalem, indeed, was crushed
   by Roman armies cruel.
Save us, dear God, from our collapse
   into indifference!

---

*Lk 19:45-20:26 = Mk 11:15-19; 27-12:17 Jesus cleanses the temple,
tells the parable of the wicked tenants, and answers the question
about paying taxes.*

We Will Live in Love Forever!

Lk 20:27-40: *Some Sadducees, those who say there is no resurrection, came to him and asked him a question, "Teacher, Moses wrote for us that if a man's brother dies, leaving a wife but no children, the man shall marry the widow and raise up children for his brother. Now there were seven brothers; the first married, and died childless; then the second and the third married her, and so in the same way all seven died childless. Finally the woman also died. In the resurrection, therefore, whose wife will the woman be? For the seven had married her."*

Jesus said to them, "Those who belong to this age marry and are given in marriage; but those who are considered worthy of a place in that age and in the resurrection from the dead neither marry nor are given in marriage. Indeed they cannot die anymore, because they are like angels and are children of God, being children of the resurrection. And the fact that the dead are raised Moses himself showed, in the story about the bush, where he speaks of the Lord as the God of Abraham, the God of Isaac, and the God of Jacob. Now he is God not of the dead, but of the living; for to him all of them are alive." Then some of the scribes answered, "Teacher, you have spoken well." For they no longer dared to ask him another question.

To contemplate:

Is marriage just a passing thing?
   Will not our dearest temporal love
      endure an eternity?

We seem to find within ourselves
   some trace of everlastingness,
      a "soul" that will not die.
But what about soul-partners, Lord,
   will they not remain as one in love
      through all eternity?

Ah, love will last beyond our years
   for the resurrection children,
      God's children in Jesus Christ.

If our Father is the God of love,
   those who live in love will never die—
      they will live on with him.

In him their love will crystallize
   into eternal love for him,
      the God of all the living.
For, like the patriarchs of old,
   we will not be dead but truly live
      in the God of all the living!

Lk 20:41-21:19 = Mk 12:35-13:13 Jesus' question about David, his denunciation of the Pharisees, praise of the widow who gave of her poverty, and discourse about the last days.

Hold Up Your Heads!

Lk 21:20-28: *"When you see Jerusalem surrounded by armies, then know that its desolation has come near. Then those in Judea must flee to the mountains, and those inside the city must leave it, and those out in the country must not enter it.... For there will be great distress on the earth and wrath against this people; they will fall by the edge of the sword and be taken away as captives among all nations; and Jerusalem will be trampled on by the Gentiles, until the times of the Gentiles are fulfilled.*

"There will be signs in the sun, the moon, and the stars, and on the earth distress among nations confused by the roaring of the sea and the waves. People will faint from fear and foreboding of what is coming upon the world, for the powers of the heavens will be shaken. Then they will see 'the Son of Man coming in a cloud' with power and great glory. Now when these things begin to take place, stand up and raise your heads, because your redemption is drawing near."

To contemplate:

Two great events you here predict, my Lord:
the Romans' destruction of old Jerusalem
and your own glorious return as the Son of Man.

The first of these dramatic prophecies
was seen fulfilled within some forty years.
The Romans trampled Jerusalem,
destroyed the temple and crucified Jews
in a nightmarish orgy of brutal tyranny.

Your second prediction has yet to be fulfilled;
the time has not yet come,
when you will return to earth in glorious power.
Fulfillment of your first forecast, my Lord,
lends credence to your second prophecy
of roaring seas and signs in sun and moon,
when time itself will drown in eternity,
as you, my Lord, take over all the world
in reign of heavenly grace and majesty!

Those who believe in you, who hope and love,
will stand and take part in your resurrected glory.
O Son of Man, come on your cloud for me!

Lk 21:29-33 = Mk 13:28-31 "Watch for the signs of the coming end of the world."

Be Alert!

Lk 21:34-38: *"Be on guard so that your hearts are not weighed down with dissipation and drunkenness and the worries of this life, and that day catch you unexpectedly, like a trap. For it will come upon all who live on the face of the whole earth. Be alert at all times, praying that you may have the strength to escape all these things that will take place, and to stand before the Son of Man."*

Every day he was teaching in the temple, and at night he would go out and spend the night on the Mount of Olives, as it was called. And all the people would get up early in the morning to listen to him in the temple.

To contemplate:

"Do not let your heart be trapped
    in the worries of this life.
Guard your mind against temptation,
    destructive fragmentation.
Live each day in the light of God,
    for it may be your last;
sleep each night in his holy arms,
    far from all that harms."

You warn us, Lord, to be alert
   against the drunken trance
that threatens to enervate our strength
   and catch us in its grasp.
At all times you would have us pray
   to rise above the things
that otherwise would drag us down,
   drag us from you, Lord.
O Son of Man, you showed us how
   to stand up to our trials;
each day you taught the temple crowds,
   each night you prayed alone.
And thus prepared, you faced the end,
   the goal of your whole life—
with your Father on the Olive Mount
   you prepared for Calvary.

Each night I too must watch and pray
   to spend each day for you
in the work that you have given me
   to advance our Father's cause.
And thus I may still hope to stand
   with you, O Son of Man!

Lk 22:1-13 = Mk 14:1-2; 10-16 Jewish leaders plot to kill Jesus; the disciples prepare for the Passover.

The
Passion
and
Resurrection

"This Is My Body, My Blood!"

Lk 22:14-20: *When the hour [for the Passover meal] came, he took his place at the table, and the apostles with him. He said to them, "I have eagerly desired to eat this Passover with you before I suffer; for I tell you, I will not eat it until it is fulfilled in the kingdom of God." Then he took a cup, and after giving thanks he said, "Take this and divide it among yourselves; for I tell you that from now on I will not drink of the fruit of the vine until the kingdom of God comes." Then he took a loaf of bread, and when he had given thanks, he broke it and gave it to them, saying, "This is my body, which is given for you. Do this in remembrance of me." And he did the same with the cup after supper, saying, "This cup that is poured out for you is the new covenant in my blood."*

To contemplate:

O Jesus, I hear you say those grace-filled words:
   "I have eagerly desired to eat
   this Passover meal with you
      before I suffer."

Moses observed the covenant
   with a solemn ritual meal
      before the Exodus.
You inaugurate your loving covenant
   with a meal of your own making:
   bread and wine you change
      into body and blood—
      your body and blood!
Your body, to be sacrificed in death for us;
   your blood, poured upon the cross!
   O Jesus, you give yourself
      wholly for us—
      wholly to us.
Moses solemnized the covenant in blood,
   the blood of sacrificed bulls.
   Now you solemnize
      by pouring blood—
      your own blood!
How you must love us to nourish us with yourself!
   In our physical act of receiving you,
   we are spiritually one with you
      in loving communion—
      Holy Communion.
   I welcome you into my silent heart—
      marveling!

The Greatest Is the One Who Serves

Lk 22:21-30: *"But see, the one who betrays me is with me, and his hand is on the table. For the Son of Man is going as it has been determined, but woe to that one by whom he is betrayed!" Then they began to ask one another, which one of them it could be who would do this.*

A dispute also arose among them as to which one of them was to be regarded as the greatest. But he said to them, "The kings of the Gentiles lord it over them; and those in authority over them are called benefactors. But not so with you; rather the greatest among you must become like the youngest, and the leader like one who serves. For who is greater, the one who is at the table or the one who serves? Is it not the one at the table? But I am among you as one who serves.

"You are those who have stood by me in my trials; and I confer on you, just as my Father has conferred on me, a kingdom, so that you may eat and drink at my table in my kingdom, and you will sit on thrones judging the twelve tribes of Israel."

To contemplate:

Even as the hand of your betrayer
    is on the table with your own,
and as the others spar for greatness,
    you confer on them a kingdom.

One of these betrays your cause;
    all the rest succumb to pride.
You warn the betrayer of the price;
    you teach the proud to serve.

All have misunderstood your way;
    they haven't come to serve, as you.
Yet for standing by you in your trials,
    you confer on them a kingdom!

And there, you promise, they'll feast with you
    and sit on glorious thrones
in the kingdom of your Father.

Judas will die and be replaced,
    but all the rest will learn to serve
as the judges of your New Israel—
    great leaders of your Church!

O Jesus, Lord of your Father's kingdom,
    admit me to his kingdom, too!

I Have Prayed for You

Lk 22:31-34: *"Simon, Simon, listen! Satan has demanded to sift all of you like wheat, but I have prayed for you that your own faith may not fail; and you, when once you have turned back, strengthen your brothers." And he said to him, "Lord, I am ready to go with you to prison and to death!" Jesus said, "I tell you, Peter, the cock will not crow this day, until you have denied three times that you know me."*

To contemplate:

First you call him "Simon."
    Is he turning back to be
        the faithless fisherman
            you found on Lake Galilee?
Since temptations in the desert,
    you've been at war with Satan.
        Will he win now in the end,
            turning your wheat to chaff?
What will happen now, Lord,
    after your cross-bound death,
        if your faithful leader Peter
            loses his faith in you?

Will your sacrifice of life
   be lost upon the world?
     Will Satan nullify
       your death upon the cross?
To prepare your future Church,
   you've prayed to brace his faith;
     though he'll deny you thrice,
       he'll never lose his faith!

Simon, you've much to learn
   before you can strengthen the rest.
     Your pride will need much humbling
       before you can be the rock.
As your Lord foretells to you
   the depths to which you'll sink,
     he will call you again, Peter,
       call you back to him!
Ready to go to prison
   and even to death with him?
     You'll finally die for him,
       but you will deny him first!

O Jesus, I, too, waver—
   may I finally stand with you!

It Is Enough!

Lk 22:35-38: *He said to them, "When I sent you out without a purse, bag, or sandals, did you lack anything?" They said, "No, not a thing." He said to them, "But now, the one who has a purse must take it, and likewise a bag. And the one who has no sword must sell his cloak and buy one. For I tell you, this scripture must be fulfilled in me, 'And he was counted among the lawless'; and indeed what is written about me is being fulfilled." They said, "Lord, look, here are two swords." He replied, "It is enough."*

To contemplate:

Why are you changing your instructions, Lord?
   When first you sent your twelve abroad,
      and later your seventy,
   you forbade them to provide for needs;
yet now you tell them take both purse and bag.
You command them even to sell their cloaks for
swords,
   and you quote Isaiah's prophecy
      that you will be disgraced!
   Are you calling them to defend you now,
to save your reputation by means of force?

They have been reading the signs of growing crisis,
   signs of the plots against you, Lord,
      the plots to take your life.
   From under cloaks they draw two swords—
now they are ready to stand and fight for you!
For three long years they have been following you;
   yet they do not understand the kind
      of war you wage for them.
   They still think like the world you grieve;
they see only the surface of events engulfing them.

"Enough," you cry—two swords to win your cause?
   Or enough to convince you that your men
      have still not understood?
   Enough of reasons, enough of words—
only acts now count, acts to save the world!
But first, surrender to the Father's will—
   You will lead them into the garden now,
      the garden of your agony.
   They'll see the uselessness of swords,
understand their need to use the sword of truth.

O Lord of Truth, let me wield your sword of truth.
   It must be enough for me!

Father, Not My Will but Yours

Lk 22:39-46: *He came out and went, as was his custom, to the Mount of Olives; and the disciples followed him. When he reached the place, he said to them, "Pray that you may not come into the time of trial." Then he withdrew from them about a stone's throw, knelt down, and prayed, "Father, if you are willing, remove this cup from me; yet, not my will but yours be done." Then an angel from heaven appeared to him and gave him strength. In his anguish he prayed more earnestly, and his sweat became like great drops of blood falling down on the ground. When he got up from prayer, he came to the disciples and found them sleeping because of grief, and he said to them, "Why are you sleeping? Get up and pray that you may not come into the time of trial."*

To contemplate:

As he goes again to the Olive Mount,
    "the disciples follow him."
Is Luke suggesting we follow him,
    even to his agony?

"Father, remove this cup from me;
  yet not my will but yours!"
Father, he loves you even more
  than he loves his own dear life.
Father, of what cup does he speak?
  Of Isaiah's "cup of staggering" (51:22),
the cup of suffering for our sins—
  anguish our sins cause you?
O Father, take the cup from him;
  spare him his precious life!
You send an angel to strengthen him,
  and he prays more earnestly—
so earnestly, he sweats great drops,
  like blood upon the ground.
Ah Father, hear his prayer for us,
  his saving prayer for me!

He finds his disciples fast asleep
  in the deep sleep of grief.
His word to them? "Get up and pray,
  pray in your time of trial."
Jesus, I pray in my time of trial,
  I pray for a part with you,
that I may stand straight up with you
  to embrace our Father's will.
For he wills not the cup of staggering;
  he wills salvation's cup!

Jesus Touched His Ear
and Healed Him

Lk 22:47-53: *While he was still speaking, suddenly a crowd came, and the one called Judas, one of the twelve, was leading them. He approached Jesus to kiss him; but Jesus said to him, "Judas, is it with a kiss that you are betraying the Son of Man?" When those who were around him saw what was coming, they asked, "Lord, should we strike with the sword?" Then one of them struck the slave of the high priest and cut off his right ear. But Jesus said, "No more of this!" And he touched his ear and healed him. Then Jesus said to the chief priests, the officers of the temple police, and the elders who had come for him, "Have you come out with swords and clubs as if I were a bandit? When I was with you day after day in the temple, you did not lay hands on me. But this is your hour, and the power of darkness!"*

To contemplate:

Rapid action now takes place:
    Judas leads the crowd
and advances to his master's side,
    greets him with a kiss.

The kiss of death, betraying kiss—
    Jesus uncovers stealth:
Ah, Judas, do you now betray
    the Lord who offers life?

Then, out with sword and vicious swing,
    an ear to pay for him,
an ear of a slave for the world's great Lord—
    how just an interchange!
Out of this chaos, Jesus speaks:
    "No more violent acts!
No need for work of swords or clubs—
    no protest to God's will!"
Out of this chaos, Jesus acts:
    as they come to capture him,
he takes out time for the wounded man,
    heals his dangling ear.
Don't they see the miracle?
    Don't they care at all?
No more than for his other cures,
    no more do they care now!

He submits himself to their custody,
    lets them shackle him.
"It is your hour," he says to them,
    "and that of Satan's power."

    O Jesus, heal *our* violence!

The Lord Looked at Peter

Lk 22:54-62: *Then they seized him and led him away, bringing him into the high priest's house. But Peter was following at a distance. When they had kindled a fire in the middle of the courtyard and sat down together, Peter sat among them. Then a servant-girl, seeing him in the firelight, stared at him and said, "This man also was with him." But he denied it, saying, "Woman, I do not know him." A little later someone else, on seeing him, said, "You also are one of them." But Peter said, "Man, I am not!" Then about an hour later still another kept insisting, "Surely this man also was with him; for he is a Galilean." But Peter said, "Man, I do not know what you are talking about!" At that moment, while he was still speaking, the cock crowed. The Lord turned and looked at Peter. Then Peter remembered the word of the Lord, how he had said to him, "Before the cock crows today, you will deny me three times." And he went out and wept bitterly.*

To contemplate:

Ah, Peter, rock of faith in Jesus Christ,
could you not answer true a servant-girl,

say "Yes, I follow the man they're questioning;
    in fact, I am the leader of his band"?
A few hours ago you boasted you would die
    rather than deny your undying love for him!
And now, not once, not twice—three separate times
    you deny you even know this blessed man
you've loved not one, not two—three blessed years.
    You could not spend an hour with him in prayer;
you could not keep them from arresting him.
    Yet, at a safe distance, you followed them,
hoping to see what they would do with him—
    no doubt, you even hope to rescue him.

By the fire you sit, awaiting any chance;
    you cannot let this girl preempt your plan,
nor the men who afterward discover you—
    you deny you even know the Son of Man.
And then the sound, the awful cockcrow din.
    You look up and see the Lord watching you;
his steady gaze cuts deep into your soul
    and touches the broken cord within your heart.
Recalling what he said, you weep hot tears.

Dear Lord, even in your most desperate plight,
    you find a way to reach the heart of the man
whom you have chosen to be the rock of strength
    for those now wavering in their faith in you.
    O Jesus, move me to repentance, too!

Son of Man and Son of God

Lk 22:63-71: *Now the men who were holding Jesus began to mock him and beat him; they also blindfolded him and kept asking him, "Prophesy! Who is it that struck you?" They kept heaping many other insults on him.*

When day came, the assembly of the elders of the people, both chief priests and scribes, gathered together, and they brought him to their council. They said, "If you are the Messiah, tell us." He replied, "If I tell you, you will not believe; and if I question you, you will not answer. But from now on the Son of Man will be seated at the right hand of the power of God." All of them asked, "Are you, then, the Son of God?" He said to them, "You say that I am." Then they said, "What further testimony do we need? We have heard it ourselves from his own lips!"

To contemplate:

"A prophet are you—a holy prophet?
   Then prophesy who struck you!"
Thus they shout in mockery,
   striking your blinded face.

You rescued Peter with a glance,
  but now you cannot see.
You saved disciples from the sea,
  but drown in misery.

With day the peoples' elders meet,
  looking to condemn.
They have their plan, they've set the trap:
  "Are you Messiah, then?"
They think they know just what you'll say;
  they know how they'll respond.
A mockery is the trial held,
  a mockery of God!

You know they won't believe in you,
  but you answer with the truth—
you are Daniel's Son of Man (Dan 7:13)
  who will sit on high with God.
"Son of Man! Then Son of God?"
  they know they've got you now.
Your own answer now condemns you—
  they simply ratify!

O Son of Man and Son of God,
  I do believe in you!
O Lord of all our suffering,
  enfold me in your heart!

I Find Nothing against Him

Lk 23:1-7: *Then the assembly rose as a body and brought Jesus before Pilate. They began to accuse him, saying, "We found this man perverting our nation, forbidding us to pay taxes to the emperor, and saying that he himself is the Messiah, a king." Then Pilate asked him, "Are you the king of the Jews?" He answered, "You say so." Then Pilate said to the chief priests and the crowds, "I find no basis for an accusation against this man." But they were insistent and said, "He stirs up the people by teaching throughout all Judea, from Galilee where he began even to this place."*

When Pilate heard this, he asked whether the man was a Galilean. And when he learned that he was under Herod's jurisdiction, he sent him off to Herod, who was himself in Jerusalem at that time.

To contemplate:

"We found this man perverting our nation."
    Thus they pervert his words—
The Son of God has taught God's people
    to disobey great Caesar!

But Pilate's spies have heard him say,
    "Give Caesar what is his."
Pilate knows that they accuse with lie—
    so what of their second charge?

"Jesus, you claim to be a king?"
    Pilate takes "You say so"
as a noncommittal negative:
    "This man is innocent."
Ah, Pilate you misinterpret him;
    with Jewish reservation
he lays his claim to be the Christ,
    King of all the kings!
Yet you are right in part at least:
    he speaks the honest truth,
and so commits no perjury—
    yes, he is innocent!

They will not let it rest at that:
    "He stirs the people up!"
Yes, he makes them think and pray;
    most dangerous is he!

Oh, Jesus stir us up again—
    Stir up my penitence;
stir up my faith and stir my hope;
    stir up my love for you!

Jesus Gives Herod No Answer

Lk 23:8-12: *When Herod saw Jesus, he was very glad, for he had been wanting to see him for a long time, because he had heard about him and was hoping to see him perform some sign. He questioned him at some length, but Jesus gave him no answer. The chief priests and the scribes stood by, vehemently accusing him. Even Herod with his soldiers treated him with contempt and mocked him; then he put an elegant robe on him, and sent him back to Pilate. That same day Herod and Pilate became friends with each other; before this they had been enemies.*

To contemplate:

The king of all the world is dragged
   before this petty king
and treated like a cheap magician—
   "Work a wonder and go free!"
Herod is king by Caesar's will,
   not by his own merits;
yet he presumes to judge the Lord
   he fails to recognize.

Ah, Herod, what will you have to say,
   when you come to your own end
and appear before the throne of him
   you judge on this, your day?
You ask him question after question;
   he answers not a one.
No, Herod, you deserve no answer,
   nor any miracle!
And so you treat him with contempt
   and dress him like a clown.
Too weak to make your own decree,
   to Pilate you send him back.

O Lord, they make a fool of you,
   these high and mighty men!
These former enemies, now friends
   in shedding blameless blood.
Dear Lord, I contemplate you there,
   standing in mocking robe,
the butt of king's and soldiers' jokes,
   the laughingstock of men!
When I stand upon my dignity
   and flaunt some tawdry feat,
let me remember you, my king,
   standing in defeat.

What Evil Has He Done?

Lk 23:13-25: *Pilate then called together the chief priests, the leaders, and the people, and said to them, "You brought me this man as one who was perverting the people; and here I have examined him in your presence and have not found this man guilty of any of your charges against him. Neither has Herod, for he sent him back to us. Indeed, he has done nothing to deserve death. I will therefore have him flogged and release him."*

Then they all shouted out together, "Away with this fellow! Release Barabbas for us!" (This was a man who had been put in prison for an insurrection that had taken place in the city, and for murder.) Pilate, wanting to release Jesus, addressed them again; but they kept shouting, "Crucify, crucify him!" A third time he said to them, "Why, what evil has he done? I have found in him no ground for the sentence of death; I will therefore have him flogged and then release him." But they kept urgently demanding with loud shouts that he should be crucified; and their voices prevailed. So Pilate gave his verdict that their demand should be granted. He released the man they asked for, the one who had been put in prison for insurrection and murder, and he handed Jesus over as they wished.

To contemplate:

"I have found this man to be innocent;
   so, I will have him flogged"—
the logic of worldly authorities
   is a travesty of truth.

"Release him? No! Release Barabbas,
   a mere rebel and murderer!
But Jesus teaches a dangerous creed;
   he demands too much of us.
Crucify Jesus—pour out his blood!
   Crucify God's Son!"

"Why, tell what evil he has done,
   so I can have him flogged!
Not happy? Well then, crucify him!
   Will that be enough for you?"
Strict conscience must be satisfied.
   How else can right be done?
The murderer is now set free;
   the healer will be killed:
thus will the justice of this our world
   be richly satisfied!

O Jesus, standing abandoned there,
   what a burden you must bear:
although you have come to save
   you are condemned to death!

Do Not Weep for Me
but for Yourselves

Lk 23:26-31: *As they led him away, they seized a man, Simon of Cyrene, who was coming from the country, and they laid the cross on him, and made him carry it behind Jesus. A great number of the people followed him, and among them were women who were beating their breasts and wailing for him. But Jesus turned to them and said, "Daughters of Jerusalem, do not weep for me, but weep for yourselves and for your children. For the days are surely coming when they will say, 'Blessed are the barren, and the wombs that never bore, and the breasts that never nursed.' Then they will begin to say to the mountains, 'Fall on us'; and to the hills, 'Cover us.' For if they do this when the wood is green, what will happen when it is dry?"*

To contemplate:

O Jesus, we watch you on your way,
   leading Simon with your cross,
but not the Simon of your choice,
   not Simon you named "Rock."

No, this is an unwilling Simon
    they force to carry your cross.
The Simon you told to carry it
    is nowhere to be found.

Only strangers help you now,
    only strangers follow you;
yet some women beat their breasts
    and openly weep for you.

You comfort those who would comfort you,
    telling them not to weep for you
but only for themselves and theirs:
    the future threatens them.
If he who brings life for all the rest
    must suffer such agony,
will not those who freely follow him
    have much to suffer, too?

O Jesus, on your way to death,
    most ignoble death of all,
you reach out to those who weep for you
    in empathy with them!

O Jesus, let me follow you,
    all your way to Calvary.
Turn your merciful face to me
    as I carry my piece of our cross.

Father, Forgive Them!

Lk 23:32-38: *Two others also, who were criminals, were led away to be put to death with him. When they came to the place that is called The Skull, they crucified Jesus there with the criminals, one on his right and one on his left. Then Jesus said, "Father, forgive them; for they do not know what they are doing." And they cast lots to divide his clothing. And the people stood by, watching; but the leaders scoffed at him, saying, "He saved others; let him save himself if he is the Messiah of God, his chosen one!" The soldiers also mocked him, coming up and offering him sour wine, and saying, "If you are the King of the Jews, save yourself!" There was also an inscription over him, "This is the King of the Jews."*

To contemplate:

They drive thick nails through trembling flesh
    and raise your cross on high;
they stand and stare at their handiwork,
    fixed there against the sky.
You gaze on them, then into gloom,
    crying out a prayer—

not of vengeance or imprecation,
    but of forgiveness rare.
You've preached forgiveness infinite,
    and now you practice it—
you implore your Father's clement love
    for your executioners!
They turn to more important things
    in utter callousness:
they try their luck to win your clothes,
    mocking your helplessness.

The people's leaders were afraid
    you might be omnipotent.
Now that they've got you hung up there,
    they mock you as impotent:
"Savior of all others, are you?
    Then save yourself this hour!"
The soldiers add their cruel taunts:
    "O great king, prove your power!"

O saving Lord upon your cross,
    you prove yourself true king
by enduring transfixed agony
    in mercy for your foes.

I embrace you there upon your cross,
    my saving Lord and king!

Today You Will Be with Me in Paradise!

Lk 23:39-43: *One of the criminals who were hanged there kept deriding him and saying, "Are you not the Messiah? Save yourself and us!" But the other rebuked him, saying, "Do you not fear God, since you are under the same sentence of condemnation? And we indeed have been condemned justly, for we are getting what we deserve for our deeds, but this man has done nothing wrong." Then he said, "Jesus, remember me when you come into your kingdom." He replied, "Truly I tell you, today you will be with me in Paradise."*

To contemplate:

Two criminals, one bad, one good,
    suffer along with you.
To the bad you are a wicked fraud,
    to the good, a most just man.
But how can a criminal be good,
    aren't they all really bad?
Yet even in the very worst of us
    is there no streak of good?

The difference lies within their hearts:
    the first holds bitterness;
but the heart of the second criminal
    overflows with penitence,
flows out to Jesus on his cross
    in sorrow for many sins,
flows out to Jesus on his cross
    in prayer for saving love.

The heart of this sorrowing criminal
    touches his sacred heart:
"This very day you'll be with me
    in God's own Paradise!"

O Jesus, you rise above your hurt,
    above your sufferings,
to hold up hope of happiness
    to a repentant criminal!
Repeatedly you've been reaching out
    to other sufferers,
even as you yourself sink down
    toward death's black emptiness.

Ah, sweet Lord of Pain and Death,
    I, too, am a sufferer;
reach out to me with promise true
    of Paradise with you!

"Father, into Your Hands I Commend My Spirit!"

Lk 23:44-49: *It was now about noon, and darkness came over the whole land until three in the afternoon, while the sun's light failed; and the curtain of the temple was torn in two. Then Jesus, crying with a loud voice, said, "Father, into your hands I commend my spirit." Having said this, he breathed his last. When the centurion saw what had taken place, he praised God and said, "Certainly this man was innocent." And when all the crowds who had gathered there for this spectacle saw what had taken place, they returned home, beating their breasts. But all his acquaintances, including the women who had followed him from Galilee, stood at a distance, watching these things.*

To contemplate:

Now all is sunk in deepest dark,
　　though it's mid-afternoon.
The curtain that hides God's majesty
　　suddenly splits in two!
No need for temple to hold God now,
　　he's here on Calvary,

listening to his dying Son
    in his final agony:
"Father, into your loving arms
    I here entrust my soul."
It is the last breath of his life,
    the end of all his acts.
His head sinks down upon his breast;
    his breast lies still in death.
His eyes stare into empty space,
    not seeing anymore.
His expressive voice is silent now;
    his arms can hold no child.
His graceful legs can't walk again;
    his face can smile no more.

The last executor of Roman law,
    the brave centurion,
pronounces Rome's concluding verdict:
    "This man was innocent!"
Too late to say this saving word—
    he's limp upon the cross.
Too late to change the march of time—
    the unthinkable's been done:
    our saving king hangs dead!

Dead Lord, into your outstretched arms
    I entrust my own live soul!

His Body Was Placed in a Tomb

Lk 23:50-56: *Now there was a good and righteous man named Joseph, who, though a member of the council, had not agreed to their plan and action. He came from the Jewish town of Arimathea, and he was waiting expectantly for the kingdom of God. This man went to Pilate and asked for the body of Jesus. Then he took it down, wrapped it in a linen cloth, and laid it in a rock-hewn tomb where no one had ever been laid. It was the day of Preparation, and the sabbath was beginning. The women who had come with him from Galilee followed, and they saw the tomb and how his body was laid. Then they returned, and prepared spices and ointments.*

On the sabbath they rested according to the commandment.

To contemplate:

Oh, the finality of death—
   irreversible separation
      from one that we have loved!

Joseph, council member
   of profound faith in Jesus,
      buries him with honor,

buries him in virgin tomb,
   as he had been conceived
      of ever virgin mother.
They bury him in haste,
   before the sabbath starts,
      the sunset of his days.

Where are his disciples?
   Must a stranger bury him,
      assisted by the women?
These ever faithful women
   contemplate his tomb,
      his dead body lying there.
On the sabbath they will rest,
   obedient to the law
      of Moses and his people.
Then they'll return again
   to complete his burial
      in last, loving service.

Now all is hushed in calm.
   I join these silent women,
      thinking quietly of him....

   O Jesus, are you really dead?

Remember What He Told You

Lk 24:1-12: *But on the first day of the week, at early dawn, they came to the tomb, taking the spices that they had prepared. They found the stone rolled away from the tomb, but when they went in, they did not find the body. While they were perplexed about this, suddenly two men in dazzling clothes stood beside them. The women were terrified and bowed their faces to the ground, but the men said to them, "Why do you look for the living among the dead? He is not here, but has risen. Remember how he told you, while he was still in Galilee, that the Son of Man must be handed over to sinners, and be crucified, and on the third day rise again." Then they remembered his words, and returning from the tomb, they told all this to the eleven and to all the rest. Now it was Mary Magdalene, Joanna, Mary the mother of James, and the other women with them who told this to the apostles. But these words seemed to them an idle tale, and they did not believe them. But Peter got up and ran to the tomb; stooping and looking in, he saw the linen cloths by themselves; then he went home, amazed at what had happened.*

To contemplate:

Something has happened at the tomb—
    the stone's been rolled away,
and his body, his most sacred body,
    is nowhere to be found.

"Why look for the living with the dead?
    He has risen into life!
Just as he said in Galilee,
    he has risen from the dead!"

Oh, message unbelievable—
    can angels tell such tales?
Yet he himself had said he'd rise—
    could they forget his words?

The women return as witnesses
    to the chosen witnesses;
but they who had seen his miracles
    still falter in their faith.

Yet Peter, who first believed in him (5:8-9),
    runs swiftly to the tomb;
he gazes at the linen cloths
    and stands amazed—dazed!

O Jesus, that's the leap of faith,
    even from death to life!
Great Lord, it is a leap I take
    to another world with you!

The Stranger Along the Way

Lk 24:13-24: *Now on that same day two of them were going to a village called Emmaus, about seven miles from Jerusalem, and talking with each other about all these things that had happened. While they were talking and discussing, Jesus himself came near and went with them, but their eyes were kept from recognizing him. And he said to them, "What are you discussing with each other while you walk along?" They stood still, looking sad. Then one of them, whose name was Cleopas, answered him, "Are you the only stranger in Jerusalem who does not know the things that have taken place there in these days?" He asked them, "What things?" They replied, "The things about Jesus of Nazareth, who was a prophet mighty in deed and word before God and all the people, and how our chief priests and leaders handed him over to be condemned to death and crucified him. But we had hoped that he was the one to redeem Israel. Yes, and besides all this, it is now the third day since these things took place. Moreover, some women of our group astounded us. They were at the tomb early this morning, and when they did not find his body there, they came back and told us that they had indeed seen a vision of angels who said that he was alive. Some of*

those who were with us went to the tomb and found it
just as the women had said; but they did not see him."

To contemplate:

Is not his face well known to them?
  They recognize him not—
just another stranger along their way,
  who knows much less than they!

We encounter him along our way
  in strangers we meet each day.
And do we see him in the face
  of those with whom we live?

O Lord, we are the ignorant ones;
  we are the ones who fail
to see the meaning of events,
  the beauty of God's plan.

Like these two on their Emmaus road,
  we stumble as if blind.
Our fragile hopes we base on dreams
  of superficial power
and merely physical redemption
  from discomforts of this world.

O Jesus, Lord of heaven and earth,
  grant us your grace of faith.
O Jesus, risen from the dead,
  we hope in you alone!

Were Not Our Hearts Burning within Us?

Lk 24:25-32: *Then he said to them, "Oh, how foolish you are, and how slow of heart to believe all that the prophets have declared! Was it not necessary that the Messiah should suffer these things and then enter into his glory?" Then beginning with Moses and all the prophets, he interpreted to them the things about himself in all the scriptures.*

As they came near the village to which they were going, he walked ahead as if he were going on. But they urged him strongly, saying, "Stay with us, because it is almost evening and the day is now nearly over." So he went in to stay with them. When he was at the table with them, he took bread, blessed and broke it, and gave it to them. Then their eyes were opened, and they recognized him; and he vanished from their sight. They said to each other, "Were not our hearts burning within us while he was talking to us on the road, while he was opening the scriptures to us?"

To contemplate:

Lord, if you should walk with us,
    would you find us slow of heart,
slow to believe in the prophecies
    that foretold your mighty deeds?

Would you find us faltering in our faith
    that your suffering has saved us?
And slow to believe in your glory, Lord,
    and the glory you offer us?

O Lord, how slow we are to believe
    the scriptures tell us true
that you are present in every one
    we meet along our way!

How slow we are to find you, Lord,
    in the breaking of the bread,
How slow to thrill to your gift of self,
    in your sacrament of love!

Our hearts know how to burn with greed
    and lust and wrong desire.
Why are we so slow to burn
    with faith and love for you?

O risen Lord, I kneel to you,
    implore your grace to love—
love you in every friend and foe,
    and your sacrament of love!

The Lord Appeared to Simon!

Lk 24:33-35: *That same hour they got up and returned to Jerusalem; and they found the eleven and their companions gathered together. They were saying, "The Lord has risen indeed, and he has appeared to Simon!" Then they told what had happened on the road, and how he had been made known to them in the breaking of the bread.*

To contemplate:

Events are moving rapidly:
    the Lord seems everywhere!

The two Emmaus travelers
    hurry back to tell the rest.
But another story preempts theirs—
    the Lord has appeared to Simon!
The two accounts of appearances
    corroborate each other.

The Lord has now restored his Rock
    from his disgraceful fall.
At supper Jesus had prophesied
    Satan would test his strength.

To become the rock for the others' faith,
    Peter had first to learn
how fragile Simon really was,
    how vulnerable by himself.

Though he had failed the test of strength,
    he turned back remorsefully;
for at his Lord's reproving glance,
    he wept repentant tears.
Then at the women's strange report,
    he ran to the empty tomb—
of all the disciples he is first
    to believe in his Lord again.

And so the Lord comes first to him,
    confirming him in faith.
From now until the end of time
    he will confirm his brothers.

Peter, confirm us in our faith
    in the rising of our Lord.
O risen Lord, remain with us,
    alive in our minds and hearts!

Peace Be with You

Lk 24:36-43: *While they were talking about this, Jesus himself stood among them and said to them, "Peace be with you." They were startled and terrified, and thought that they were seeing a ghost. He said to them, "Why are you frightened, and why do doubts arise in your hearts? Look at my hands and my feet; see that it is I myself. Touch me and see; for a ghost does not have flesh and bones as you see that I have." And when he had said this, he showed them his hands and his feet. While in their joy they were disbelieving and still wondering, he said to them, "Have you anything here to eat?" They gave him a piece of broiled fish, and he took it and ate in their presence.*

To contemplate:

Haunted by their unfaithfulness
   to their mission to follow him,
they think that they now see his ghost,
   returned to take account.

He knows exactly what they need:
    "Peace be with you all!"
Still they think they see a ghost.
    "I am not ghost but flesh!"

Though he comes and goes with spirit ease,
    he's not the Spirit yet to come,
but flesh and bone and hands and feet,
    and a body that can eat.

As so often he has done before
    he sits and eats with them.
He eats a fisherman's fare for them,
    a piece of broiled fish.

Good choice—he leaves the bones for them
    to examine when he's gone!
And when they have recovered calm,
    they'll know his flesh is real.

They saw him die upon a cross,
    his flesh torn through and through;
yet here he is with flesh anew,
    arisen from the dead!

O Jesus, risen from the dead,
    come to my table, too!

You Are My Witnesses!

Lk 24:44-49: *Then he said to them, "These are my words that I spoke to you while I was still with you— that everything written about me in the law of Moses, the prophets, and the psalms must be fulfilled." Then he opened their minds to understand the scriptures, and he said to them, "Thus it is written, that the Messiah is to suffer and to rise from the dead on the third day, and that repentance and forgiveness of sins is to be pro- claimed in his name to all nations, beginning from Jerusalem. You are witnesses of these things. And see, I am sending upon you what my Father promised; so stay here in the city until you have been clothed with power from on high."*

To contemplate:

They failed their mission to follow him
   even to the cross.
Yet now he gives them a new command:
   "Be witnesses to me!

"Give witness to the promises
  I have fulfilled for you,
the promises of the prophets true,
  who foretold my life and death.

"Give witness to my death for you
  on a cross on Calvary:
'Like a lamb that has been led to slaughter,
  he opened not his mouth' (Is 53:7).

"Thus I have won for you forgiveness
  just as the psalmist sang:
'There is forgiveness from you, Lord,
  that you may be revered' (Ps 130:4).

"Give witness to my risen flesh,
  new fellowship with you:
'On the third day he will raise us up
  to live again with him' (Hos 6:2).

"Give witness to the gift I'll send
  as promised by my Father:
'I'll pour out my spirit on all flesh' (Joel 2:28),
  my most Holy Spirit."

Lord Jesus Christ, of flesh and bone,
  I will your witness be;
O Holy Spirit, the Father's gift,
  bring Jesus into me!

He Blessed Them and Ascended

Lk 24:50-53: *Then he led them out as far as Bethany, and, lifting up his hands, he blessed them. While he was blessing them, he withdrew from them and was carried up into heaven. And they worshiped him, and returned to Jerusalem with great joy; and they were continually in the temple blessing God.*

To contemplate:

From Bethany upon a colt
   he had come in poverty
to die upon a twisted tree
   an ignominious death.

The crowd had showered him with praise
   in promise of glory great.
But within the week they turned on him:
   "Crucify our king!"

He died to free us poor of earth
   from the tyranny of sin;
He died to give us all he had—
   forgiveness from our God!

Then he rose to give us life—*his* Life—
    eternal Life with God;
he rose to send his Father's gift—
    Gift of the Holy Spirit.

Yet before he gives this Spirit-Gift
    he must withdraw from them—
free them from complete dependence,
    upon his body-presence.

He leads them back to Bethany,
    to the summit of the mount,
and begins his last triumphal march
    to the new Jerusalem.

Straight up to everlasting joy,
    carried on angels' wings
to eternal throne at his Father's side,
    his glory forever new!

O Son of Mary, Son of God,
    I, too, worship you!

Epilogue

Acts 1:12-14: *Then they returned to Jerusalem.... When they had entered the city, they went to the room upstairs where they were staying, Peter, and John, and James, and Andrew, Philip and Thomas, Bartholomew and Matthew, James son of Alphaeus, and Simon the Zealot, and Judas son of James. All these were constantly devoting themselves to prayer, together with certain women, including Mary the mother of Jesus, as well as his brothers.*

Acts 2:1-4: *When the day of Pentecost had come, they were all together in one place. And suddenly from heaven there came a sound like the rush of a violent wind, and it filled the entire house where they were sitting. Divided tongues, as of fire, appeared among them, and a tongue rested on each of them. All of them were filled with the Holy Spirit and began to speak in other languages, as the Spirit gave them ability.*

To contemplate:

Jesus' ascension does not end the story;
rather, it opens the final phase of God's plan,
the chapter of the action of the Church
guided now by Jesus' Holy Spirit.

Luke names eleven apostles faithful still,
waiting with Mary for the Holy Spirit,
waiting with her to whom first the Spirit came—
praying with her who first brought forth the Lord.

For now they, too, will bring the Lord to all.
But first they must be filled with his new life,
reborn in him through his most Holy Spirit,
in violent wind and burning fire of love.

The creating Spirit hovered over chaos (Gen 1:2)
to order all things into nature-oneness;
now the Spirit hovers over them
to create them anew in spirit-oneness.

O Holy Spirit of wind and fire and flame,
rouse our minds to faith in Jesus' thoughts,
enkindle in our hearts his greatest hopes,
inflame in our spirits his all-embracing love.

Give us a tongue that can proclaim to all
the kingdom we grasp by faith and hope and love,
the heavenly kingdom of our Father-God,
the new Jerusalem where Jesus dwells
in union with the Father and with you—
      lead us to eternal glory, too!

Dear Luke,

We thank you for portraying our Lord
   in his compassionate love
for all the poor, sick and distressed,
   along his saving way.

Your stories of his infancy—
   his conception from Virgin Mary,
his visit to his cousin John,
   his birth in Bethlehem,
the simple shepherds' narrative,
   his temple presentation,
his teaching in his Father's house—
   your endearing memories of him.

The Holy Spirit leads him through
   temptations in the desert,
his rejection by his own hometown,
   and by religious leaders.

Yet he preaches love of enemies,
   restores life to a widow's son,
holds up as example a Samaritan
   who cares for a wounded Jew.

He reveals our God as a loving Father
of a worthless prodigal son
as well as a jealous, miserly son—
the children that we are.

Luke, you show him kind to women,
little respected in his day;
you show his choice of humble sinners
over the pretentious proud:
the woman who wiped his feet with tears,
the beggar who ate his master's crumbs,
the tax collector who beat his breast,
Zacchaeus who repaid his debts.

And thanks for detailing his afflictions
on his path to Calvary,
and his final glorious resurrection
and ascension to his Father.

O Jesus,
We would walk life's journey along with you,
beginning as did the shepherds
who followed the angels' song from on high,
to find you in Mary's arms.

We would accompany you along the road
from Galilee to Jerusalem,
listening to your teaching true,
your proverbs and parables.

With Martha we would learn to work
   in the presence of your peace;
with Mary we would learn to pray,
   just listening at your feet.

With Peter, Andrew, James and John,
   and all your men and women,
We would walk the long, long road with you,
   the road to Calvary.

You suffered your passion and death for us,
   yet still had thought for others—
for the servant who almost lost an ear,
   for Peter who denied he knew you,

for the women who mourned as you
   carried your cross,
   for the soldiers who crucified you,
for the good thief who defended you,
   for all of us who believe in you!

Then into your Father's loving hands
   you offered up your spirit.
And on the third day you rose again,
   living a life all new!

We would walk along the road with you,
   the high road to Emmaus,
the road on which you teach God's Word,
   and stay to break the bread.

BOOKS & MEDIA

The Daughters of St. Paul operate book and media centers at the following addresses. Visit, call or write the one nearest you today, or find us on the World Wide Web, www.pauline.org

CALIFORNIA
3908 Sepulveda Blvd., Culver City, CA 90230; 310-397-8676
5945 Balboa Ave., San Diego, CA 92111; 619-565-9181
46 Geary Street, San Francisco, CA 94108; 415-781-5180

FLORIDA
145 S.W. 107th Ave., Miami, FL 33174; 305-559-6715

HAWAII
1143 Bishop Street, Honolulu, HI 96813; 808-521-2731

ILLINOIS
172 North Michigan Ave., Chicago, IL 60601; 312-346-4228

LOUISIANA
4403 Veterans Memorial Blvd., Metairie, LA 70006; 504-887-7631

MASSACHUSETTS
Rte. 1, 885 Providence Hwy., Dedham, MA 02026; 781-326-5385

MISSOURI
9804 Watson Rd., St. Louis, MO 63126; 314-965-3512

NEW JERSEY
561 U.S. Route 1, Wick Plaza, Edison, NJ 08817; 732-572-1200

NEW YORK
150 East 52nd Street, New York, NY 10022; 212-754-1110
78 Fort Place, Staten Island, NY 10301; 718-447-5071

OHIO
2105 Ontario Street (at Prospect Ave.), Cleveland, OH 44115; 440-621-9427

PENNSYLVANIA
9171-A Roosevelt Blvd., Philadelphia, PA 19114; 215-676-9494

SOUTH CAROLINA
243 King Street, Charleston, SC 29401; 843-577-0175

TENNESSEE
4811 Poplar Ave., Memphis, TN 38117 901-761-2987

TEXAS
114 Main Plaza, San Antonio, TX 78205; 210-224-8101

VIRGINIA
1025 King Street, Alexandria, VA 22314; 703-549-3806

CANADA
3022 Dufferin Street, Toronto, Ontario, Canada M6B 3T5; 416-781-9131
1155 Yonge Street, Toronto, Ontario, Canada M4T 1W2; 416-934-3440

¡Libros en español!